High Performance Price Action Trading

Monetize your knowledge in reading the charts candle by candle

Dainius Šilkaitis

ISBN:151434730X
ISBN-13: 978-1514347300

DEDICATION

I dedicate this book for my wife Sonata. She is the most important people in my life, I am always feeling her support and love. She always inspires me and that's the reason why I decided to share my experience at the markets. Without her love, persistent guidance, care and support nothing have been possible.

CONTENTS

PREFACE

For many years, I have wanted to write the book about my personal experiences in trading Price Action system. I believe that there are no better systems to trade successfully than Price Action trading. Take a look at the charts from the past – come back to the ages when Jessie Livermore and other masters traded. What's the difference between it and nowadays? Nothing. The same price action moving the markets. There are the same two forces, which try to take over control at the market. The same human psychological forces working every day with the charts. Only the market price is our chief – we must listen to it and follow the price action. As a speculators, we need to use trend following strategies, but better to use other term – market price following strategies. Because about 60-70 percent of the time the price is moving in non-trending environment, only 30 percent of time we see strong trends. As a trader you can't be stubborn or arrogant, there is no place for your individual ego. As Jessie Livermore said: ,,Speculation is nothing more than anticipating coming movements." In order to anticipate correctly, one must have a definite basis for that anticipation.

At this book I will show you my personal breakthroughs in trading Price Action. I have tried a lot of systems since I have found the power of the Price Action trading. For now I am listening to the market every single day and doing results from trading. If someone would offer me that information at the beginning of my trading carrier, I think that my way to trading success would be much more easier. At this book you will find the different look at the market and understand what professional traders were seeing at the market that you couldn't see.

Standard technical analysis methods won't make you money. You can't just do what everyone is doing. You need to be smarter than the crowd. Every time you try to execute the order at the market, you must ask yourself some questions, also see the perspective from bullish and bearish side. Why professionals traded here? Why You couldn't see the signal at the same place? At this book I will show you how to read the ,,tape'' of the market bar by bar, candle by candle. I suppose that if you understand me correctly, your trading will be better and better every day. That's my real motivation, because I believe that every people deserve to live better. Good habits are the prequel to happiness.

Enjoy my trading ideas and become consistently profitable trader

1. MARKET DEVELOPMENT STAGES/PHASES

Every trading day must start with your determining of Market Phase. At his section I will help you to understand about MARKET Phases based on Price Action analysis and that they mean in trading. Sometimes traders use a lot of indicators, Fibonacci, other tools in their trading, but are disappointed of them. Nothing works better than price action. You don't need to see the charts similar to Christmas tree (with many decorations), because it does your trading more complicated, affect confusion mood and also usually gives you late signals.

My trading is without indicators – just follow price action. It is only truth method in trading – less noise, more concentration to charts, follow price action candle by candle. Price is my boss, I must follow and understand that it tells me. The best indicator in trading is your mind and knowledge. Your result in money is the result of your knowledge. If you play basketball at the highest level, you don't calculate money – money comes to you automatically. And you don't need to be the best basketball player, you need to be just good and play at the high level. The markets are the same business as others, but there you don't need to be good boss – you must read the tasks and execute them from your boss – the market price. Trader is people who needs to develop ability to listen the market and execute at the right time and at the right place, understand market movements correctly.

First of all, let's understand the environment where we are trading: financial markets are full of prepared participants, algorithms and individual traders, whose are doing more than 5 trillion dollar turnover every day. If you want to BUY, other institutions also should BUY at the same moment, because it is the main condition for the price uprising. Where are a lot of algorithmic trading – high frequency trading. And algorithms are making huge turnovers every day. Before trading successfully, you must understand trading environment. Algorithms are trading simple, basic strategies. In small channels, ranges volumes are huge, because algorithms doing huge volumes and open, close positions every single second. One system is BUYing, other Selling at the same time. When one makes money, other losses. That's how market works. And this works 24 hours a day, 5 days a week. Algorithms are very fast – for that reason they are named as High Frequency Trading systems. Servers are very fast, systems trade in small time frames – orders duration sometimes is less than 1 second. So they are scalping for small profits – sometimes few pips, but doing thousands of trades every day. We can't compete with that systems. Only one people who I know can do it. His name Paul Rotter, he also known as ,,the flipper''. This guy has phenomenal reaction, unique trading style, which is based on price action. By some accounts, he was trading as many as 180.000 contracts per day in 2005. That made him the largest trader of German debt futures on the Eurex. I think it is not good idea to trade in M1 charts or smaller, unless you have phenomenal reaction. In my opinion and method, that helped for me to earn stable returns in trading, I use mostly M15 chart for the entry, sometimes M5. We can see that big players or institutions are doing every day – price action shows us it on every moment. My goal is to show you how enjoyable trading that is based on following price action. Every situation, that works in M1 chart is working in Weekly, monthly charts. Sometimes people whose don't understand trading emphasize the fact that the markets sometimes crash.

It is weekly chart of EUR/USD – huge crash from 2014 MAY till 2015 March. For me it doesn't look horrible, because I can see the same Price Action every day in smaller time frames or other charts:

For example, Crude OIL Daily chart from 2014 September till 2015 January:

There is GBPUSD M15 Chart of 2015 January:

USD/CAD M1 Chart:

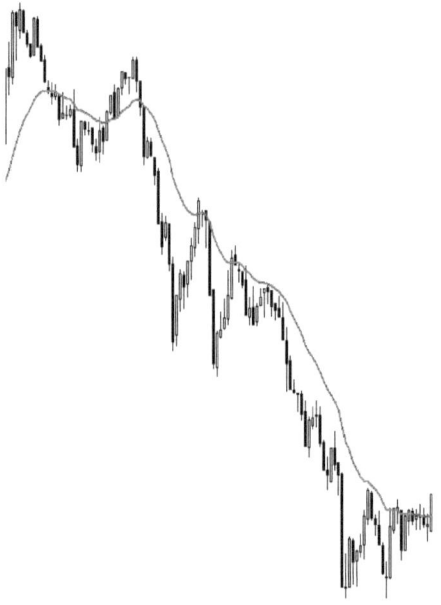

20 Mar 12:33 20 Mar 12:49 20 Mar 13:05 20 Mar 13:21 20 Mar 13:37 20 Mar 13:53 20 Mar 14:09 2

What's the difference between these charts? You can search the same situation also in Bonds, Currencies, Stocks, Commodities. Every day could be crashes in M1 chart. You must be prepared. So the most valuable system that you could learn in trading or longer time investing – ability to read price action. For me, it is not important what to trade – there are no difference, all markets are speculative, so working in the same principles – fear and greed. Forex, stocks, bonds – the same principles of Price Action works in all financial markets. Algorithms are made by people, so working by rules, that people set them – use moving averages,... Read the tape as it did Jessie Livermore (Reminiscences of a Stock Operator) and your knowledge help you monetize as much as possible from the markets. There are no bad days to trade – every second someone BUYS, someone SELLS. Your goal is to be at the right place and at the right time and read the instruments that you can recognize.

95 percent of volumes at the market are made by institutional players – hedge funds, banks, hft trading firms. Only 5 percent of volumes are made by individual retail speculators. When one side wins, other side lose the

money at the same moment. If retail speculators won't work, the markets exist the same as now. One institution BUY, other SELL. Sometimes one wins, sometimes other. There are always 55/45 percent probability. For that reason forex market is also known as zero sum game. Monetize from the markets only players, whose are using proper capital management rules. In this book, I will tell you how it is better to use probabilities and proper capital management rules. It is one of the most important rules that I have learned during my career and achieving my goal to do trading my main source of income. And now my goal is achieved – market pays me high income. My human duty is to reveal and share Price Action methods that really matters from the heart. I suppose that some people will grasp it and turn in positive results. From my experience – the only truth in trading or investing is Price Action reading. My opinion about indicators and other methods are really skeptical. I think that you will understand why...

The markets are always the same. What's the difference between nowadays and historical charts? Sometimes I like to analyze historical charts and see that price action is the same as it is now, because people behavior the same – fear and greed emotions markets mirrors every single day.

Retail traders can't move the market and affect price action!

What is High Frequency Trading?

It is automated trading type, that makes the most volumes in the markets (60-70 % of volumes). They are scalping for small profits and have minimal effect to price direction during the day. Typically, those firms execute 10-15 million orders every day, average 3000-4000 financial instruments in portfolio. Probability 50-55 percent and the most crucial factor is money management rules. Other institutions make 25 percent of volumes and retail traders 5%. So we can't move the market. The markets we created by institutions for their benefit. Nowadays we can enjoy ability to trade with them also. For that reason liquidity is incredible. Every day traders must be prepared to compete with other prepared and best or good traders. Even the best traders do mistakes at the market, because Holy

Grail not exists. Possibilities are near equal for both sides every moment. For that reason we see extremely important information in charts every second/minute/hour. Don't skip through the fingers price action analysis. Price dictates trading conditions for us.

1.2. MARKET PHASES

Every trading day I start from determining what market phase I see on the chart. The best to start from bigger picture. Never ignore the bigger picture. Bigger picture helps to determine the Market Phase.

Trend usually starts from huge breakout when the price is going up or down with near 90 percent degree. It means breakout. Candle after candle make new highs/lows – the dominant force easy recognizable. Of course, the price can't go straight with high degree forever. Breakouts transform to Channels that at the beginning stage usually are narrow and steep. From time to time market try to break the channel trend line, but 70-75 percent and more attempts to reverse the market fail. Every time contrarian forces try to reverse the market, the dominant force takes control again.

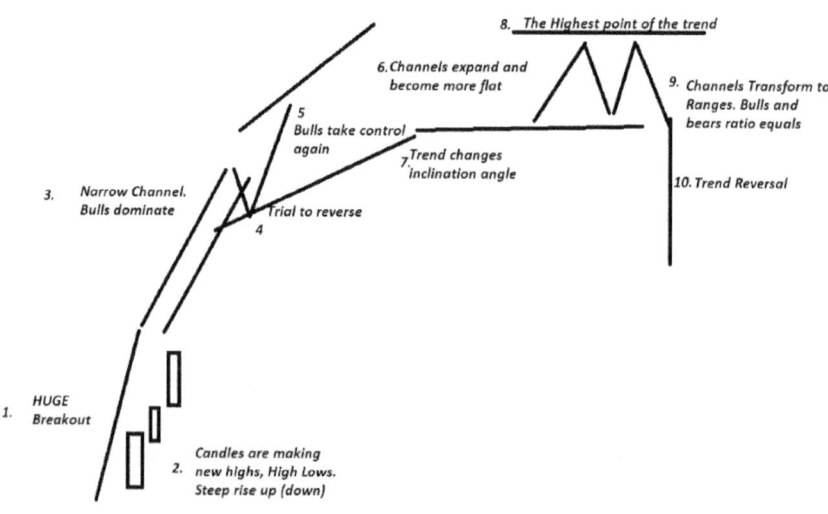

Trend finishes at the time when bulls/bears determine that the highest/lowest point is reached at the market. Usually big players like to take profits near the highest/lowest magnetic support/resistance levels. For that reason 70-80 percent and more attempts to reverse the trend fail – bulls/bears simply don't think that market reached the hottest point where could be possibilities to close long lasting orders. Usually when the market go against the trend, trend followers use that information for enter the market at the better price. Market Phases: Breakout/Channel/ Interval or in wider channels/Trend reversal. New trend breakout. As I mentioned before, there are huge amounts of algorithmic trading every second. Ask yourself in a Trend: can the algorithms understand a wave against the trend as opportunity to go against the trend? Or maybe go with the trend at the better price? Let's think about one thing: what indicators can use algorithms or most people in the charts? Moving average, trend lines, MACD, support resistance. As much the price goes up/down in the direction of the Trend, the more indicators show opportunities in direction of the trend. Does one wave against the main direction change their understanding about direction? Most of strategies are Trend Following strategies, so for that reason most algorithms and institutional players find opportunities to BUY/SELL at the better price, but in direction of the TREND.

1.3. How to determine market phase easier?

I recommend to use reliable approach that I use in my trading. Open chart and ask yourself: **Does the wave I see in front of me the trend?**

There are possible two answers: Yes or Not and your behavior depends on that.

1. If yes, you don't need to think a lot – ONLY Buy/Sell in the direction of the trend. The odds are in your favor. At this situation there no need to have a lot of sophistication – only BUY/SELL. Add BUY/SELL extra positions after corrections, keep the profitable positions as long as you can.

2. If you can't determine the direction an the chart – there is no trend. You

are at the Interval. If you are in the Interval, it is better to BUY from lows of the range and SELL highs. It means that both forces are equal in the market. There is no bullish/bearish control in the market. Both sides have ability to earn the money at this market phase or situation. There is more sophistication needed. A lot of mistakes are made by small retail traders at this stage. Only educated, experienced price action traders can generate the money in that cycles. Algorithms also do mistakes at this stage. Because as you know from your experience – lots of indicators shows us lagging signals. There is no TREND, uncertainty, visually can't determine the Trend – chances for bulls/bears near equal. It is an unfortunate truth that the markets will not Trend forever. Sometimes this amounts to a little congestion in the middle of an up (down) trend, others may be extended congestion while the market struggles to find defined direction. From my personal experience I can say, that approximately 60-70 percent of the time the prices are in Range/Interval environment. That's the reason why to earn the money is difficult.

1.4. Correction Size

As you know, at the Bull trend we are always establish Higher Highs and Higher Lows. It is normal, because bulls control the market. But we must always follow corrections of the waves, which are in the direction of the main trend. Usually, correction size depends on the inclination angle of the previous impulsive trend wave. Correction of the steep wave up/down usually finishes after one or two pushes down/up. Correction of the wave with the lower inclination angle usually finishes after three or four pushes down/up. If correction continues more, we lose the trend.

Clear direction at the chart – Bulls control the market. Trend continues after few pushes down.

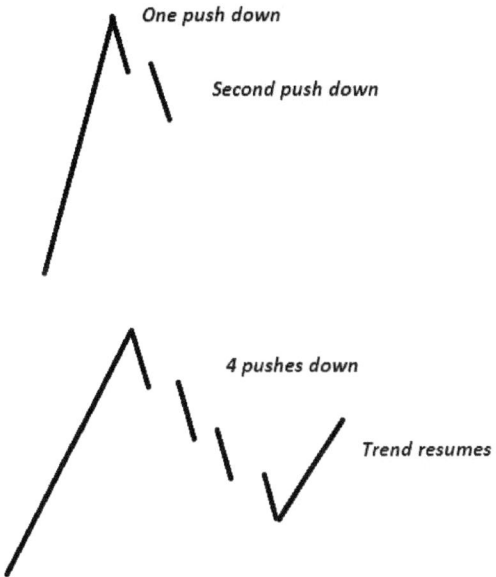

Prolonged correction: lose the trend. Market Phase – Trading Interval. BUY Lows, Sell Highs with minimal profit/loss ratio 2:1. Both sides control the market.

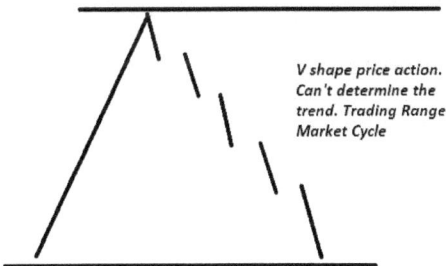

Let's think about probabilities. Probability is one of the main thing, that is unknown for us. We can't say that probability of success of the trade is 70, 80 or more percent. Probability predetermine us confusion and emotions during the trading process. I personally recommend you to do assumptions of probability on every trade. For example, I have tested a lot of automated strategies, also personal manually managed portfolio and see that all best systems don't have more than 60 percent accuracy. I personally use one reliable standpoint. When I am trading in the trend, I make assumption that have 55 - 60 percent chance of success. 60 percent chance is enough for me to feel more comfortable with the trade, so it is enough 1:1 profit loss ratio. But if I choose trade against the trend – only 35 - 40 percent maximal chance to win even the place looks good. So I need to use minimum 2:1 and better reward/risk ratio.

For example, at this situation I show you USD/CHF H1 Chart:

Bulls dominate at the market. 55 - 60 percent success probability for the trade, because it is clearly defined Bull Trend. Better to search BUY orders for any reasons. Don't wait for ideal prices, because ideal prices or trades don't exist. Sometimes people are waiting for bigger corrections, but if the trend is strong, it is possibility don't have bigger correction for a long time. If you are waiting for bigger correction, you lose the trend. BUY for any reasons, eve at the higher prices. If the price is High, BUY small positions. If correction occurs, BUY bigger positions – you don't need big stop losses. Probability is the thing that we can't control. We can manage the Lot size (volumes), stop Loss, take profit. My advice: don't wait for the best prices at the market. There are no bad prices, only bad position size. People sometimes behave in the market the same as at the shop – they want to BUY for better prices. Financial markets are different. There the price is not important – important is direction. Institutions don't like cheap prices and cheap things – they are selling more and more in a downtrend or only BUY in the UPTREND. Don't wait for discounts for doing BUY decisions. People sometimes behave differently – they need better prices or discounts and BUY for the reason, because the price is cheap and currency or stock ,,must'' go up for unknown reasons. Don't do this, because it is disastrous. Emotions – hope, fear, greed and many others can't override logic in decision making. Emotions are that motivates people to act. Emotions are normal in our lives and in trading, but we must control them. With only thoughts, and without emotions, people would spurn actions , they would lack the ,,guts'' to take risky decisions. On the other hand, when emotions kill reasoning, the probability of mistakes becomes quite high. Every setup in trading as a trader you must look from technical, money management and psychological perspective. In other sections I will show you importance of that. Because in trading nothing like money into the slot of the human thinking machine to activate its gears. Decision to BUY or SELL a financial asset belongs to decision under risk and uncertainty.

If the price are at the Range, probability is equal for bulls and bears – 50/50 percent. Both of forces have the same chances. As you see at the picture, it was big correction down and the price came back to the beginning of the upside movement. So we see V shape price action. It means Interval.

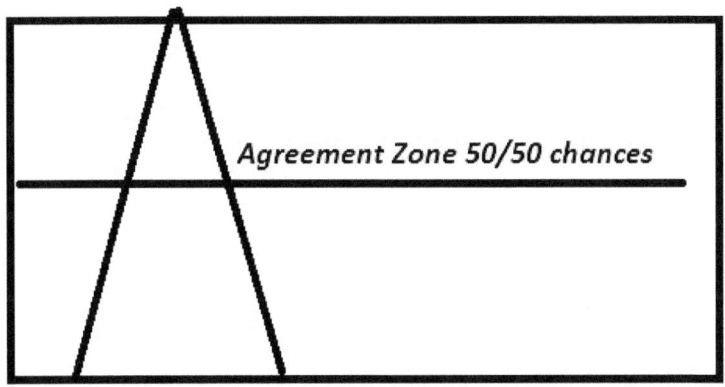

Agreement Zone 50/50 chances

Let's imagine situation from life: Do you bravely take a risk if have probability only 50 percent? I think not. But If the market can offer you 2:1 and better reward/risk ratio – that's different situation and different behavior. So if the price now is at the center of Interval – don't BUY/SELL, because risk/reward can be only 1:1 if you enter at the chart you see V shape price action. You have 50 percent probability and only 1:1 risk/reward ratio. It is irrational to BUY at this point. If you want to BUY at this point, you need to go to the lower time frame that shows you clear trend and BUY with small risk and the same reward.

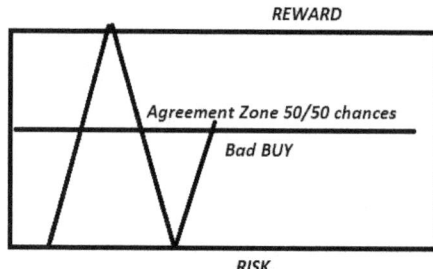

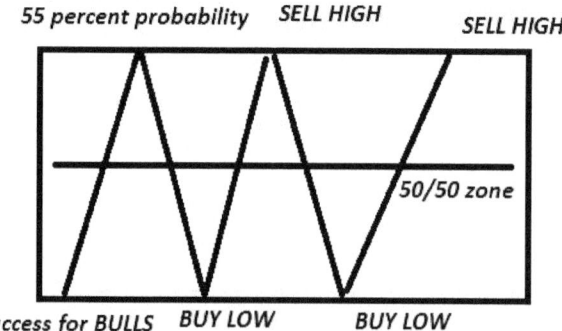

As far as the market goes to the highest/lowest point of the range, probability of success increases to 55 percent. And risk/reward ratio also increases. So you are going near the best places to execute orders. If you look at the same situation from smaller time frame perspective, you can wait for bigger and bigger corrections or Trend Reversal signals of the small trend as the price goes near the highest/lowest point of V shape.

Let's imagine other scenario: do you bravely take a risk if have probability only 40 percent? I always get for trade against the trend maximal 35 - 40 percent probability. And it helps me don't feel comfortable in trading against the trend. Minimal reward/risk ratio must be 2:1 and more. What's the reason to BUY/SELL against the trend if take 1:1? It is irrational. And people in financial markets usually do a lot of emotional, but not rational decisions. That's the real problem. It is your money, you must behave with them not as in casino, it is not a game. It is your job and you must be rational.

1.5. Why we need to know the Market Phase?

It is different opportunities to trade in different market conditions. Market changes constantly, so you must identify and alternate your opinion if it is needed. Your business conditions dictate the market. A clever trader is an observer more than a participant. Regardless of circumstance, he will remain neutral and observant, paying equal attention to the forces that oppose his potential trade as to those in favor of it.

AUD/NZD Chart:

What do you see in that chart? Remember: First of all, you must answer to

1 magical question before taking the action: Is this a TREND?

1. **If yes, look for only BUY/SELL opportunities.**
2. **If not, it is bullish/bearish wave in Trading Interval.**

What answer do you choose? I think that every people, even new at the markets choose correct: 2 answer – Wave in Interval.

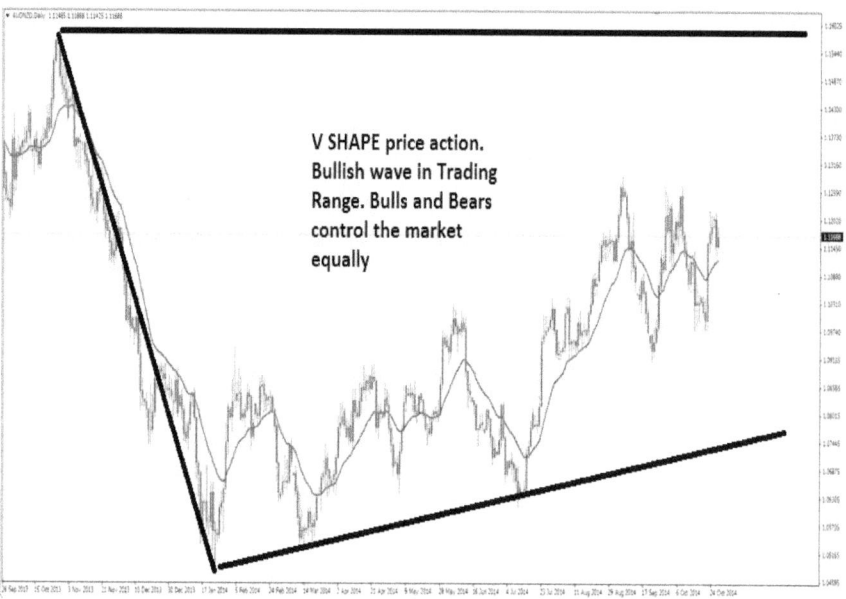

V SHAPE price action. Bullish wave in Trading Range. Bulls and Bears control the market equally

V Shape Price Action. What Market Cycle does it means? It means Trading Interval. You can't diagnose the trend easy, market lose the trend. No clear direction.

REMEMBER: every second at the market there are bulls and bears. One side is buying, second is shorting. You must follow the price if need to be successful trader.

Look at the chart from Bullish perspective:

Common mistake: people think that Bullish wave is the trend and waiting for correction (use Fibonacci, other tools, that usually shows BUY signal at that place) for BUY. Professional traders and institutions see V shape price action there in a downtrend. It is longer correction, because price came back the same path that went down before. And at the highest point of V shape it is good potential for institutions SELL with good reward/risk ratio. Chance of 55 percent and reward/risk more than 1:1. Bulls are buying with 1:1 reward/risk ratio, but possibility at the highest point only 45-50 percent. It is irrational and common mistake. Sometimes can be successful to do that, but if you do that always, don't wonder if your portfolio decrease. Your goal in the markets is to learn behave rationally.

The same situation from Bearish perspective: At the same time exists BUY and SELL orders every second. This situation is not an exception. Sellers has better probability and also better Reward/Risk (about 1,5:1). They don't chase the market. No one indicator can show you better than price action

At this situation and usually both of forces – BULLS and BEARS are profitable. Whose of them are more profitable in LONG term?

Common Mistakes of Bulls:

- Follow the bullish wave as a trend. You must determine the end point of that wave (micro Trend in smaller timeframe) and prepare for action in opposite direction.

- 1 – it is not correction.

- X-A wave is Bullish wave at the downtrend.

- V Shape formation means transformation to Trading range (Interval).

WRONG TOOLS from classical technical analysis:

- All tools and indicators can work good if are using in correct place/market phase and correct time.

- Fibonacci. Wave X-A is not trending wave. Fibonacci shows the signal from 38 level. But Stop Loss must be below 78,6, profit less than till 0. Bad Reward/Risk ratio.

- 20 EMA (exponential moving average). The price is above 20 EMA. Don't BUY. Market is not trending!

Rules at the TRADING RANGE:

- BUY at the lowest points.

- Sell at the highest points.

- Probabilities at the trading range:

- 50/50 percent. Both bullish and bearish pressure. Earn money together.

- Success key: 2:1 profit loss ratio.

What is going NEXT?

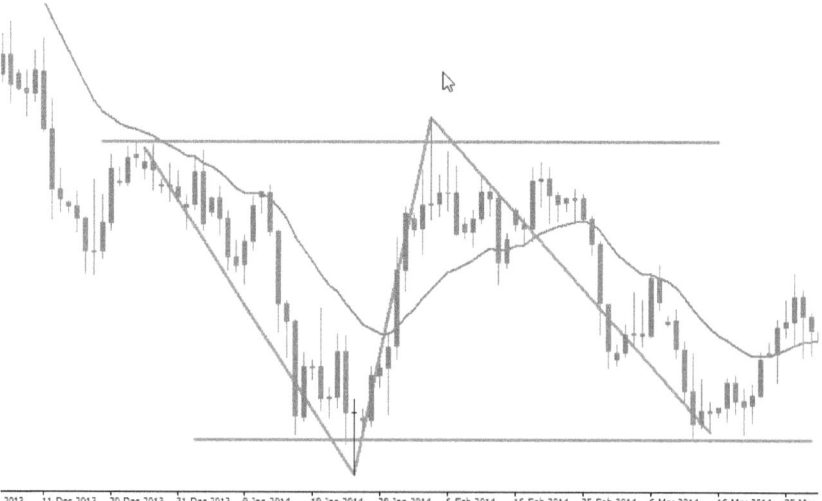

Bearish wave. What trend do you see at the chart?

Is it bear trend or bear wave at the Range/Interval?

Bearish perspective and tools that is used:

- Micro Trend Line, 20 EMA.
- SELL Decision based on emotions. Wrong news,...

- Trading is your Business. Does this trade is good from business perspective?

What makes trading as a business? MONEY.

You should understand that this is not a book on basic technical analysis. It is a book
about comprehensive price action trading approach that I have found. It is not candlestick analysis, it is market behavior in each situation analysis. Reward/Risk as in all business are the most important.

At this point bears have bad reward/risk ratio and probability 50 percent or less. Institutional BEARS are waiting for breakdown of Interval for sell. At this point they took profit from SELL HIGH orders.

Bullish perspective: the same possibility (little bit higher – near 55 percent), but there is Profit higher than possible Loss:

What's next?

- Higher Highs and HL at the TR.

- Does this Upwave TREND?

Let's look at the chart from bullish perspective: Risk 2 times bigger than Reward. It means trap for Bulls. Probability 45 -50 percent for bulls. Irrational to BUY:

The same picture from bearish perspective: SELL high. Reward/Risk 2:1. It is business deal. Take that!

Trading Interval: BUY LOW. Can expect Higher Low than previous wave lowest point, because Higher Lows market forming in Trading Interval:

First Loss in Trading Range: Sell High order finished with Loss.

Breakout of an Interval. What Market Cycle is now? TREND. Only BUY

False Breakout. Loss. The price came back to Interval. Don't delay and go for short:

Sell at the HIGH of Trading Range with 2:1 ratio:

Is this a downtrend? It is bearish wave in Interval. BUY LOW. Good Reward/Risk ratio. Don't SELL, because it is not downtrend:

BUY second position above 20 EMA. It is the bears trap, because they expected that before was downtrend:

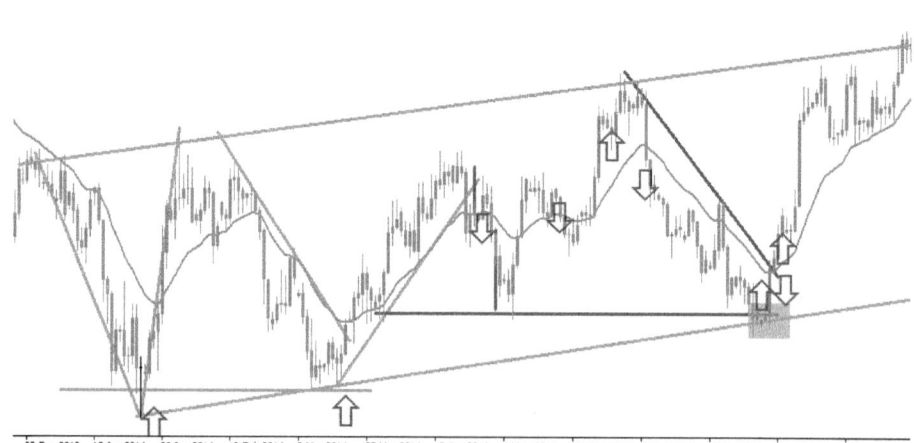

Is it Bullish Trend or wave in Interval? RULES: BUY LOW, SELL HIGH.

SELL – better Risk Reward.

This time bears fail. Remember: It is not exact science – it is the art of probabilities. 55 - 60% Success ratio – your goal. Don't be afraid of 40% probability of failure. It is normal. It is part of your business.

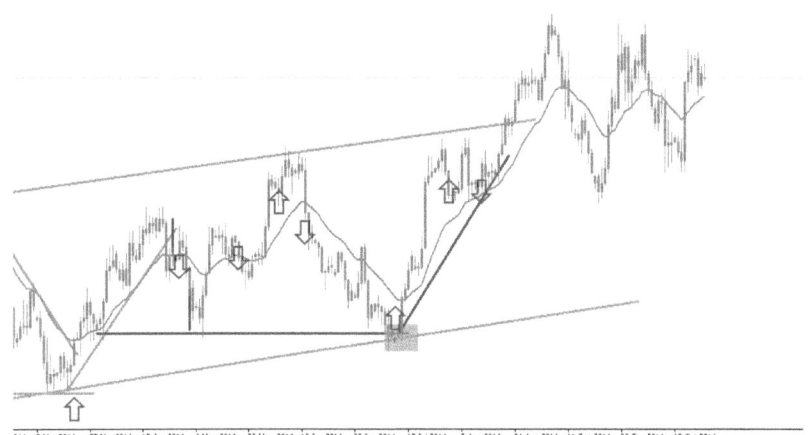

What's Next? Breakout of INTERVAL.

My thoughts is about Bullish trend . Bullish trend in smaller timeframe.

Look for BUY opportunities in smaller time frames:

Market PHASE. TREND: BUY with 1:1 reward/risk. 60 percent chance of success. The odds in your favor:

Don't forget to look at the bigger picture! What's the market phase in Daily Chart? Is this upward movement a trend?

How much trends do you see at the chart? Bigger picture shows that bulls price action is micro trend (short term trend) at the bigger TR.

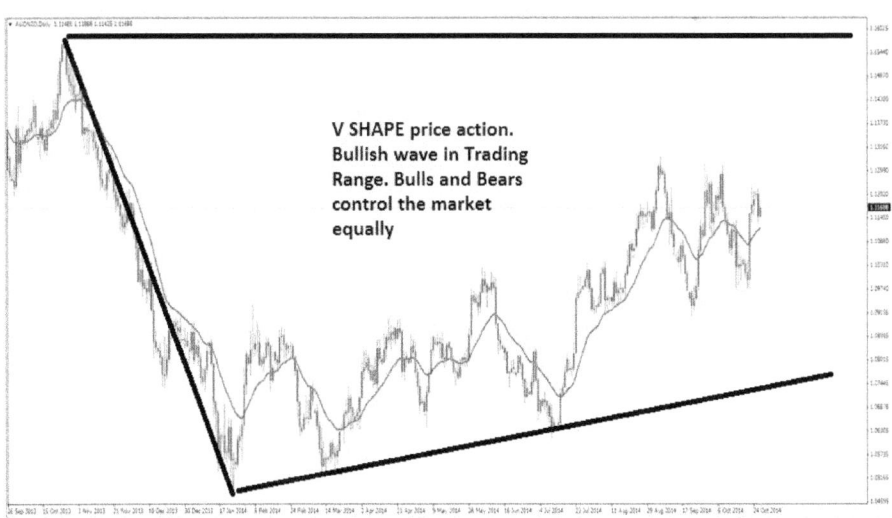

What do you think about X-A wave? Is it a downtrend? It is bearish wave in TR.

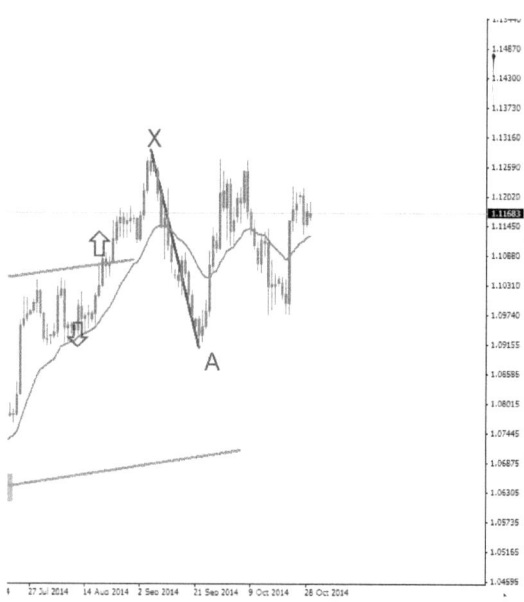

What do you do? V shape pattern. BUY LOW Probability 55 percent. Reward/Risk 2:1.

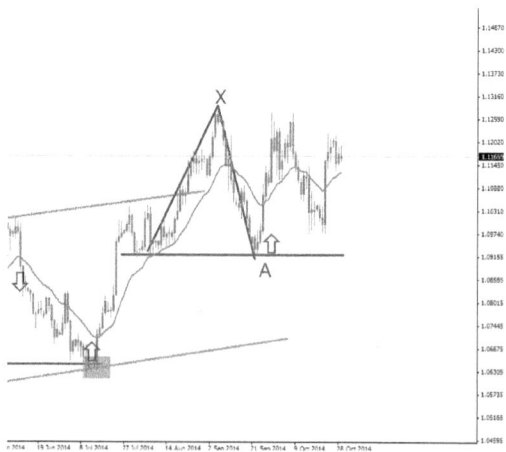

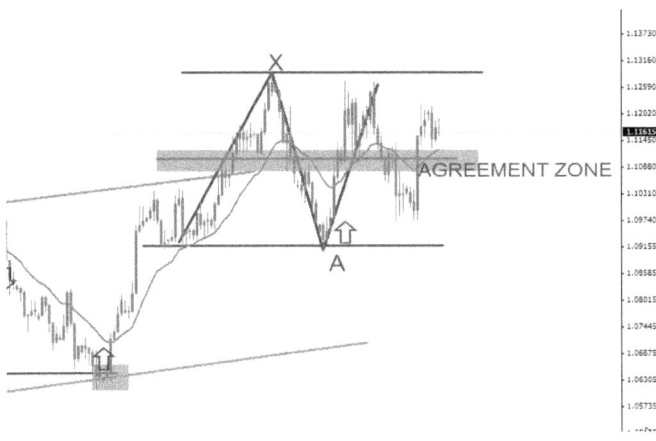

Sell HIGH: 55 percent probability. Reward/Risk near 2:1. Bears took control from BULLS:

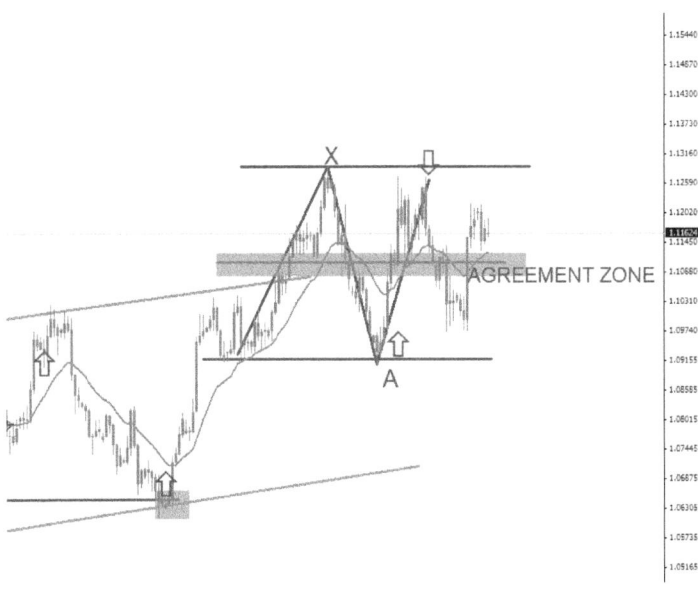

BUY on the dips. Remember: your job is to follow the institutions, follow PRICE ACTION. Higher Lows and Lower Highs. Market Phase: Trading Interval.

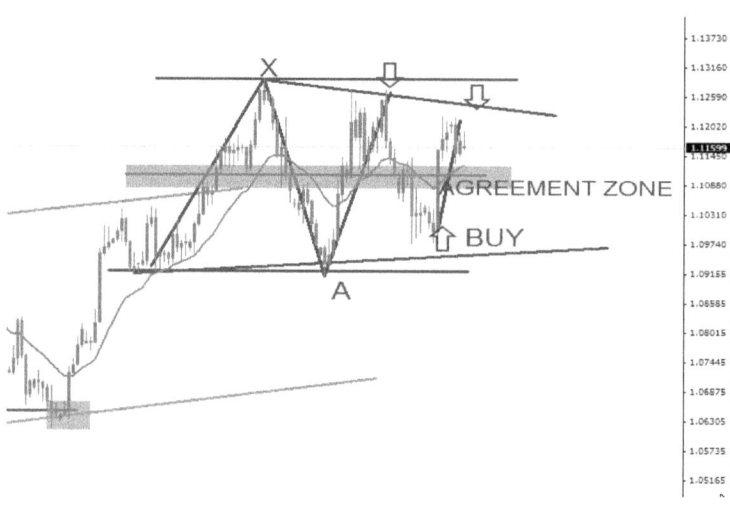

FORECAST: As far as price going up to Interval Top at the Daily chart, probabilities for Sellers increase to 55 percent. Also as much as price is moving higher, better Risk/Reward ratio for Sellers.

1.6. CONCLUSION from MARKET Phase lesson:

Keep it simple. If you see more than 1 TREND at the chart – Trading Range (Interval) market Phase. Think about probabilities also. It is about 50 percent. Trading is a business. Reward/Risk Ratio – KEY to success. Remember question before every trade execute: Is this a Trend? If Yes, follow it, only BUY/SELL for any reasons. If Not or difficult to determine, you are in Trading Range.

Bear trend. Decision: ONLY SELL.
Sell at the market price, sell after corrections, keep profitable positions as long as possible. Trending environment:

Your Business:

- Probability Assumptions.
- 60 percent or near that success ratio is your goal.
- Reward/Risk no less than 1:1 on every trade. Because if you are trading with smaller reward/risk, you need to keep 70 percent success ratio. It is impossible for a lot of traders. Your goal is not to be correct, your goal is to earn money. By scrupulously identifying the market phase, you know up front your reward/risk criteria. You know up front whether or not you wish to participate

in a given trade or wait for the next opportunity which is always just around the corner. Loss of opportunity is preferable to loss of capital.

Bull Trend:
BUY at the market price, BUY after corrections, keep profitable positions as long as possible. Trending environment:

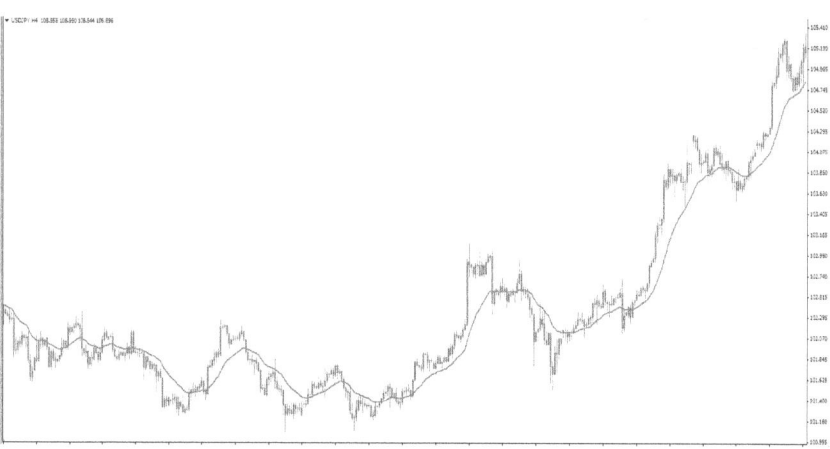

There is no difference that financial instrument you trade: Price Action always dictate you conditions and follow them. In other sections, I will learn you to recognize more situations and price action at the chart.

Remember: successful traders take their trading very seriously. They fully understand of doing business and accept the loses that came with the job. They don't talk about magical indicators. Trend, range, market phase, market sentiment – the main tools. You must be as a business man, trading is your business. Control your risk, have realistic goals and meet success in the markets. Also don't forget the alternations: they aren't stubborn. If market conditions change, change your plan. Always ask yourself: what I see on the market? What is the market phase? Is it a Trend or Interval?

2. WHO CONTROLS THE MARKET AT THE MOMENT?

Price Action shows us every day the dominant force in the market – bulls or bears. As I mentioned in section before, every second opportunities exist in the market: someone is buying for some reasons, someone is selling. So every trade you must see from Bullish and Bearish perspective. Bulls try to form Higher Highs and protect the lows. For that reason Bulls don't let for bears to form Lower Lows and Lower Highs.

Before start your trading day, you must read the information that chart is telling you. One of the main things in my system is to determine who controls the market? There are always about equal number of BUYERS and SELLERS at the market.

I like to use 20 Exponential Moving Average as indicator of the strength of trend. If the price brokes 20 EMA in smaller chart, it means that the price can go to 20 EMA in bigger timeframe.

Large BULL Bars creates buying pressure

Greater Chances of HIgher prices

What's the reason not BUY?!

A lot of traders, whose don't earn at the market, wait for better prices to entry the market or bigger corrections. Greater chances of higher prices in clearly defined Trending market phase. People usually wait for better prices. The greater the chances to win at the trade, the greater the risk – wider stop loss is needed. We can't control probabilities. As always, the better probability and profit opportunities, the bigger risk. It is typical on every business.

Always ask yourself: what to do? Who controls the market? If you consider what to do – choose order that match the direction. Follow the controllers of the market. If wider Stop Loss is needed, chose smaller position size.

Bear Trend:

Bull Trend:

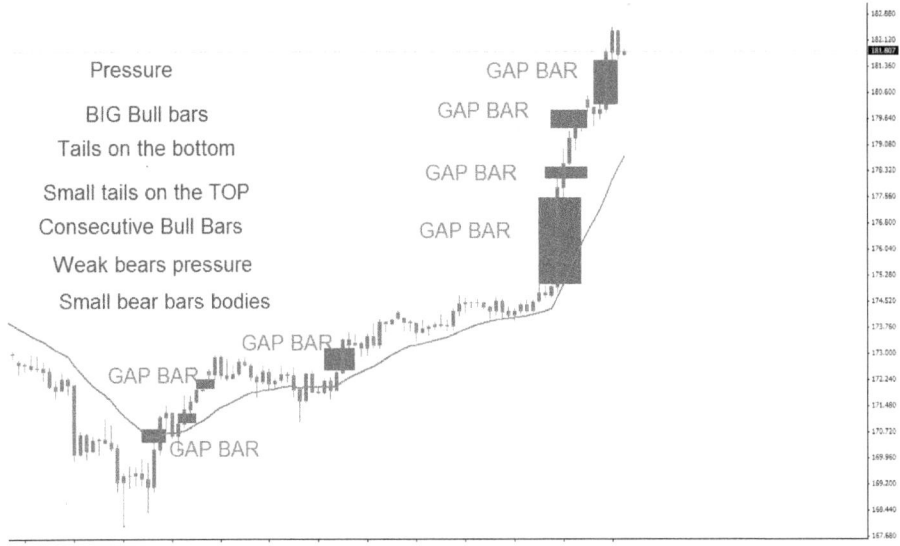

Pressure

BIG Bull bars

Tails on the bottom

Small tails on the TOP

Consecutive Bull Bars

Weak bears pressure

Small bear bars bodies

Ranges/Intervals: Both sides earn the money. Carefully follow the price action in Interval. What force is trying to dominate at the market more? Follow Higher Highs, HL, LH, LL.

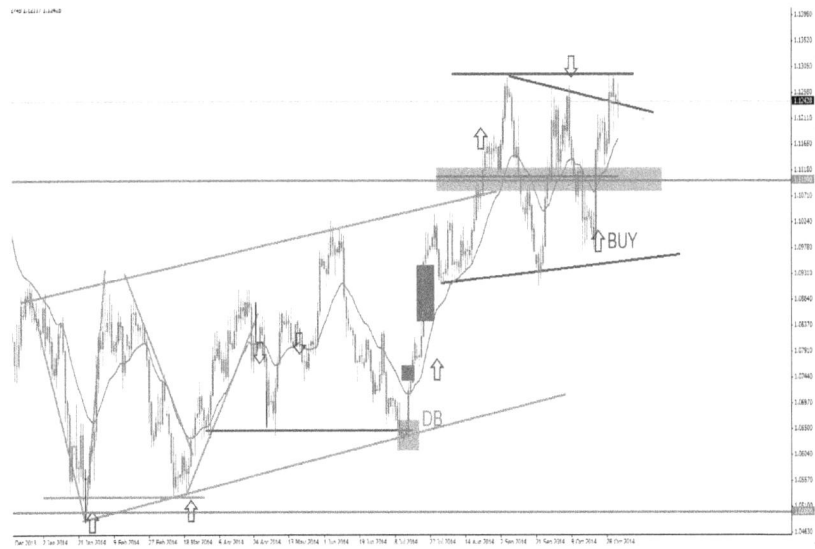

Bears take control in TR:

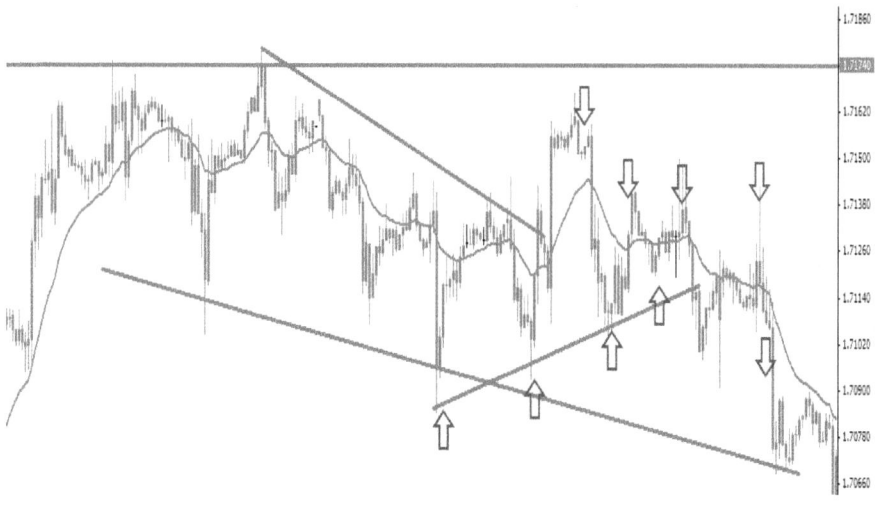

Trading range with increasing Bullish pressure. Wait for Trend Reversal signal – breakout from trading Range.

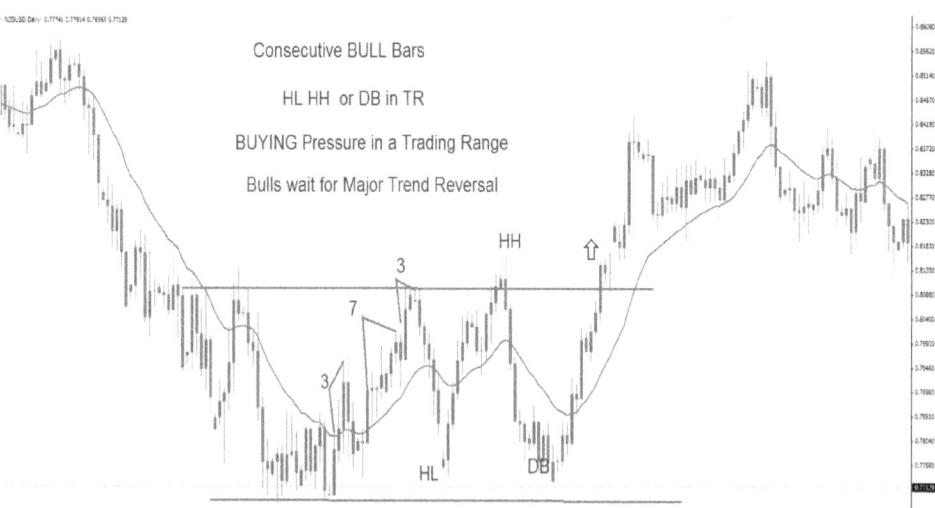

Strong Breakout:

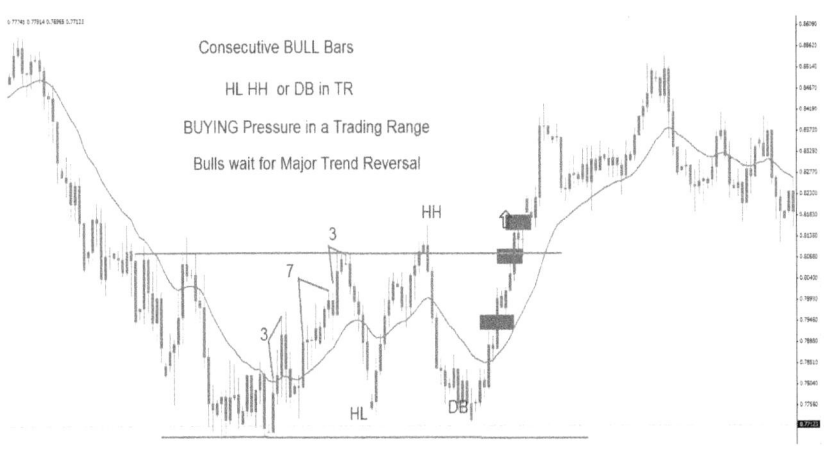

Bullish pressure:

Smaller timeframe: Interval Trading. BUY at the LOW

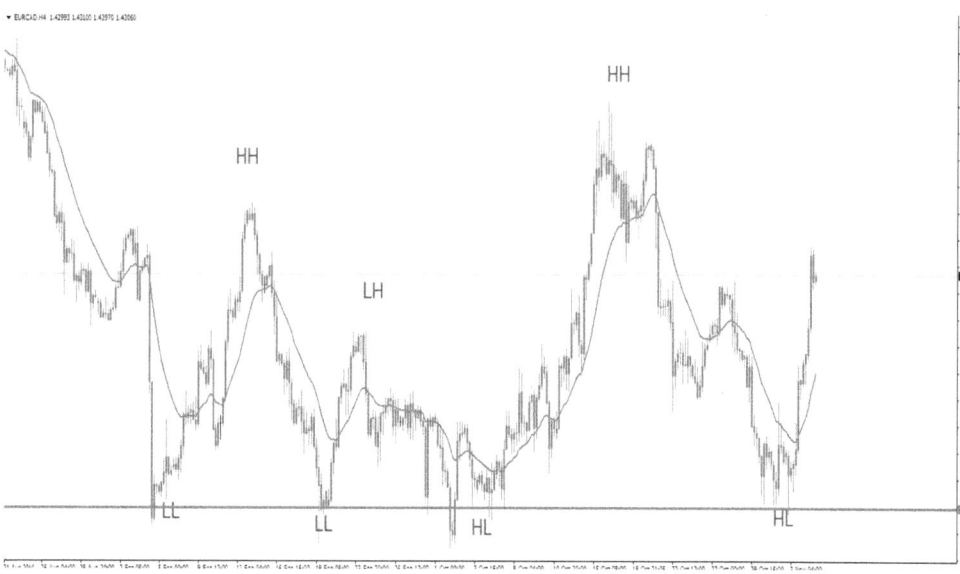

Smaller timeframe of the same chart. Bulls took control at the bottom of the interval/range:

2.2. Who controls the market in Channel?

Channels usually are part of the TREND. If we see steep rising channel, it means that Bulls control the market. Don't trade against the trend, because more than 70 percent attempts to reverse fail. If the price breaks trend line of the channel, usually market transforms to Intervals (ranges), but doesn't mean that the price change direction.

Sellers pressure in a Bull Channel:

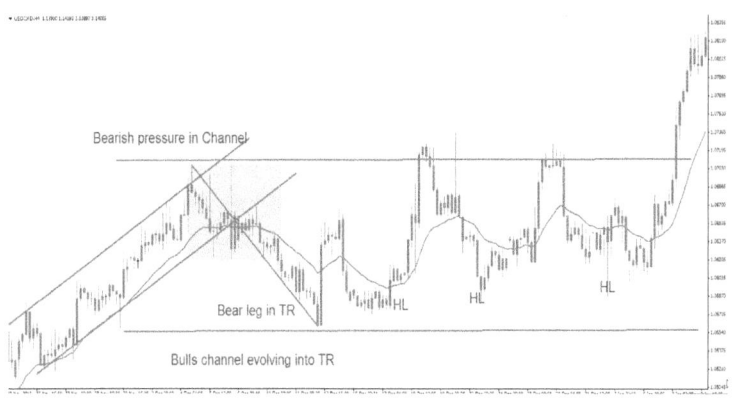

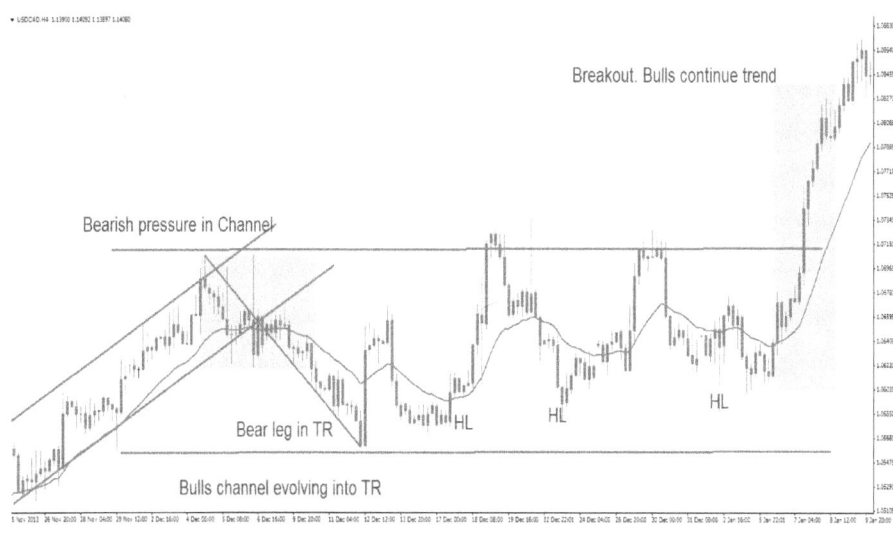

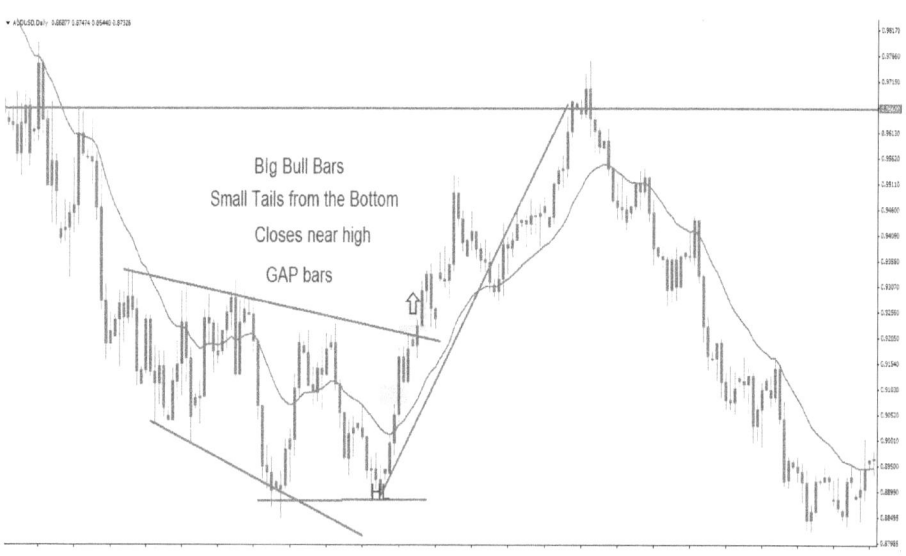

Big Bull Bars

Small Tails from the Bottom

Closes near high

GAP bars

Bear in mind:

- No edge will ever make a trader beat the market.

- The market is not a beatable object.

- Proper education – your ticket to constinently profitable results.

- True edge in the market – your ability to exploit the incompetence of others.

Price Action dictate all conditions in the market. There are no miracles, it is not as lottery – only your knowledge affect your trading results. Your edge is not just strategy. It is the sum of all knowledge and skills. In your trading bussines, you are your edge. If 90 percent of traders are net losers, for that reason you need work on skill development more than 90 percent of other traders.

3. HIGH PROBABILITY TRADING AFTER NY OPENING TIME

Psychology and nervous, not stable mental attitude to the charts comes from unknown environment. Probability is always unknown thing for trader. Probability causes emotions in our trading. Sometimes for that reason traders don't capitalize the best opportunities at the market. Entry places always look not good enough for taking the trade.

During my 10 years career at the market, I've found one interesting thing that want to share with you. This helps me to erase emotions from trading. My foundation is that the Highest or the Lowest point of the day (day start point from NY open) forms at the 3 first hours then NY opens. First of all, I've started to use this my view empirically, but after some time when I saw amazing results of trading that idea, I decided to analyze 10 years data of various financial instruments and I could safely say : The highest or The Lowest point of the day forms at the first 2 hours after Chicago market opens, nearly 90 percent of time.

Why this phenomenon happens?

Because the most volatile and most active market hours are at the time then London, Frankfurt, New York, Chicago market works together.

During London and Frankfurt working hours, NY join, one hour after –

Chicago. The most important market moving news releases usually are at 8 or 9 in the morning in NY time. And all the most important financial centers could adopt that information and place their trades based on that information. So it is really important to follow price action during these most active market hours and take action as early as it is possible. Your task is to determine - is it the lowest/highest point of the day? And take action based on that.

HIGH probability Strategy after NY open:

First of all, I always try to use 1:1 reward/risk ratio in my trading then use this strategy, because probability is really high. 1:1 and high probability let me feel stable emotionally during every trade I make at the market. I personally have my own view to capital management. What means in my trading style 1:1 profit/loss ratio? When we place the trade, stop loss is placed at the place that is correct technically (usually below/above the last low/high). But it is our primary risk. We don't know what's the risk of that trade will be real. So I always recommend for my students to calculate real risk of every trade. And Profit calculate based on Real Risk that were experienced.

For example, place order with stop loss of 100 pips. Take profit must be also no less than 100 pips if we are trading in the direction of the trend. But I don't think that this idea is good capital management rule. Better to see your REAL risk, that were taken during the order.

Our order were executed and first of all price goes against us. For example, 43 pips against us and after that reverse and go to our direction. So our REAL risk was 43 pips, for that reason profit target should be no less than 43 pips if our trade is in the direction of trend. If our trade was against the trend, no less that 43*3 pips profit target. I recommend to trade against the trend only at the places where profit/loss ratio is no less than 2:1 and more. Reliable view to capital management is to trade taking in consideration of REAL risk and reward based on that.

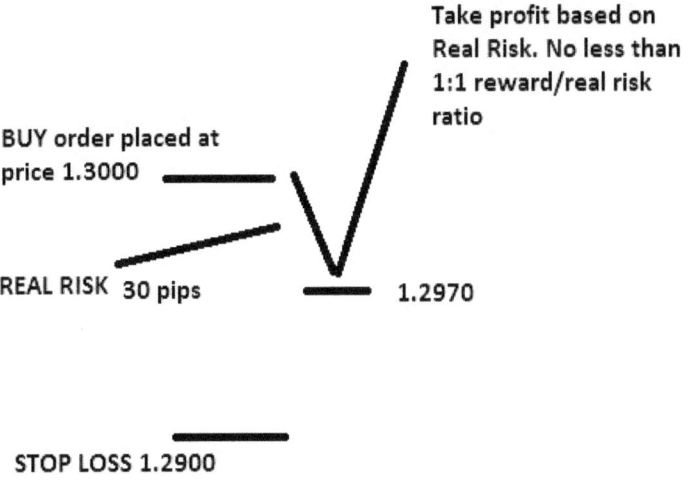

Take profit based on Real Risk. No less than 1:1 reward/real risk ratio

BUY order placed at price 1.3000

REAL RISK 30 pips

1.2970

STOP LOSS 1.2900

3.2. HIGH PROBABILITY PRICE ACTION STRATEGY AFTER NY OPEN requires no Less than 1:1 Real risk/reward ratio. For me it is reliable approach and good rule for trading with more discipline almost every day.

All strategies trader creates, he must think about Technical Setup, Money Management and last but not least Psychological Perspective. Novice, experienced as well as professional traders that execute the trade can feel more anxiety, doubt, pain and frustration. During market analyzing moment trader feel control, confidence, but after position is taken, some of this skills both with technical and money management erases. As I wrote at the beginning of the book, before starting my trading career, I was student in Music Academy. From my childhood I needed to prepare for concerts to bigger auditorium. At one moment I've been teenager, I won a lot of competitions, but after some time I felt fear of scene and my results went down. I've studied to play for about 8 hours every day then my friends played basketball. And after very good preparation I felt strong self confident, but when the concert started, I lost all these skills and showed only 10 percent of performance I was prepared. After performances, my mood was awful. After year of that performances, I and my teacher decided to improve my psychological skills. One lesson I've learned is that people must require from themselves realistic goals. My young minimalism didn't help me, because I required from me better and better – I wanted to show for all how talented I am. The same at the market – people want to beat the market. That's one of the reasons why they are not successful. Other lesson – you must practice in real market conditions every day – don't analyze history a lot. The problem is that people analyze only moments of success from history, if trade was not successful, they try to find out why. People programming themselves to learn trade with high expectancy. And then they do the trade in real time, they also believe that every of them will be successful, or even breakeven. The same is with fear of scene – if you want to fight with that, you must know the problem, but don't analyze your past, but looking only forward. My psychology trainer always required to invite friends, family members in my rehearsals. At the beginning I invited only one people, after some time more people, after some time more teachers to listen how I play. When the piece were prepared for concert, before concerts I had own rehearsals in concert halls. You must feel environment and understand that people don't push you - they are just listen and after the concert go home with their problems. You are not as important for them as you think. The same at the market – trader must train himself to trade in real time. Before every trade I must understand, that you don't need to beat the market, you don't need to be perfect. Because there are probabilities – all time you have 60/40 or 45-55 probability in your trade. Also in concert – you can do some mistakes, but if you are concentrated, don't feel fear and anxious, just need to do music – the result will be better or good. In my trading career I can use a lot of lessons from my previous experience. And it helps me to trade. And only one method that can help you feel more comfortable is reading price action candle by candle. You don't need to concentrate on the past – your view must be only forward. What market conditions offer you? My price action methods are based not only technical skills or money management, but also every setup from psychological perspective. I've learned about emotional intelligence. It is one of the most important think in our lives. Emotional intelligence we will study in other sections.

The most important parts of your mind that affect your decision making process:

1. Information: Your mind consumes information from the environment and circumstance you are in and it reacts to it. So what comes in matters. If you're around negative people, your mind wants to mirror that negativity. If you're around something inspiring, your mind mirrors that too. Forgot the loses that was made yesterday or in the past – concentrate your attention to future. Be diligent about consuming positive, intelligent, and instructive information so you strengthen a healthy, informed, positive mind.

2. Interpretation: Once your mind takes in information, it interprets it by asking, "Is this good or bad? Is this safe or dangerous? Should I approach or avoid? "Interpretation is primarily driven by past experiences, what we call conditioning. People can interpret the same information differently because they take in different parts of the information or their mind is conditioned differently from their past. Remember the rules – how do you need to act at this situation?

3. Action. Don't afraid to lose, because it is the part of your business. There are no an ideal places at the market – every time positions looks not guaranteed, because guarantees don't exist. Be self-confident and take an action immediately if market dictates you opportunity.

Our actions of yesterday form the thrust of how we think today. The more positive actions we take the more positive our minds become. Takeaway: Be around people and environments that inspire and activate the good parts of you, interpret things in positive ways, set powerful intentions, and take action so your mind feels stronger, more confident and capable.

Why I wrote about psychology in High Probability Strategy? Because this strategy helps me to be more confident at the market during first few NY and Chicago market hours. Probability is one of the things we can't control at the market.

We can control money management (reward/risk) and ourselves. That's more important than probability. But if strategy can get you higher probability, you can feel more confident.

OIL chart. Strategy requires to wait during the most volatile market hours (London, Frankfurt, NY, Chicago work at the same time). The highest or the lowest price of the remaining part of the day forms during these hours. So look from 13-16 GMT time and follow price action at this chart in M15 timeframe. Mark the interval and the highest/lowest point. Your work is to set – Is it the highest or the lowest point of the day? What shows price action? You can wait for breakout of the interval and execute after breakout – your probability is high, because if the price breaks the lowest price of interval, you know that the highest point of the day was reached and high probability look for downside movement.

I like to read price action and set the highest/lowest point from price action reading. It lets me to go for a trade earlier than after breakout of the range. At this chart number 1 shows bearish exhaustion candle – next two candles after that shows possible climax of bears. What's going next? Price comes back. Is the upward movement the trend? Not, It is the bullish wave in Two sided movement (Interval).

Number 2 candle is the biggest in up wave. It means possible bullish climax there. After that bar small bear candle – inside bar – possible preparation signal bar, and 3rd bar confirmed signal candle. SELL at the high. Stop loss better to place above the highest point of bullish candle. Prefer profit/ loss ratio no less than 2:1 at that point, because we are taking the trade at the possible highest point of Interval. After Interval closes, the price broken interval lowest point – this is notification that the highest point was at the point we've expected. Open other sell position with higher probability, but smaller volumes, because the entry price worse and bigger stop loss is needed.

Next day: Breakout price action movement. 5 strong bear candles – bears dominate at the market. Some bullish bars, then bears take control again. Sell with stop loss above signal bear bar. After interval closed, breakout of the lowest point. Sell Extra position with smaller amount, but better probability.

What's on the next days?

Next day range different. Huge bulls breakout. It looks that better to BUY and expect that the lowest point was reached and the price can continue upward movement. Don't forget to see the bigger picture! Does the movement show us bullish trend? No, it is micro trend. It is bullish wave in interval:

V shape price movement. The price is going to the high of the BIG interval.
More the price comes far from agreement zone (middle zone of the
INTERVAL), more chances for bears at that place. 4 consecutive bull bars
and after that nice signal bar for bears. Context is good, because upward
movement is only up wave inside the Interval. Sell HIGH with 2:1 ratio.
SELL HIGH later and expect for lower prices.

The price goes down and reach 2:1 profit target. Bears make lower highs
and LL. Now 13-16 GMT Interval is near possible bottom of the Bigger
Interval.

The biggest bear bar near possible bottom. Next bar has big spikes from both sides and small body. Don't BUY. Wait for more information. Next bar shows bearish strength. Wait for more – next two bars are inside bear bar. Next bar strong bull bar. BUY LOW. Expect that the lowest point was reached. Follow price action after trade is executed. Next 4 bars pushes the price lower - bears are in control. Time is near 16 GMT. Possible highest point was firmed. Close order and place sell after breakout of the Interval. SELL position compensate loss from BUY position. Don't fear to change your opinion. As early you change your opinion, at the better price you can execute orders.

Bears took control at the market. Next day the same – since NY open bears fully control the market. 6 consecutive bear candles. The last biggest bearish candle shows us possibility of exhaustion. Few bull bars and signal Bar for going Short. Stop above the signal bar. Bulls hold bottom after Interval Close Time.

Sell stopped out. Bulls signal bar near the bottom and entry bar for LONG position.

Bulls reached the profit target next day at the high of Interval.

Bears take control of the market from the high and continue domination during Interval Time. There is no signal Bar for bulls in Interval. After Interval Close time – bearish breakout and bearish signal formed. SELL and keep you order till LL and LH forms.

Next day Bears are in control. Market Phase – bear breakout. LL and LH. The same in 3 hours interval. Sell after the price breaks 3 hours Interval. Better don't leave your scalp orders opened before the weekend! Close before the weekend.

On the Monday price reversed from the high and bears pushed down to the low of previous day. Is this a trend? Not. It is bearish wave. V shape price movement. Near the bottom of Interval one of the biggest bear bars (exhaustion bar) and signal bar, after that entry bar. BUY LOW. Take profit at 1:1 reward/risk ratio.

Bears took control at the market. Bears breakout. The price stopped little bit lower than the lowest point of previous day. Traders can expect support:

V shape price action movement. One of the biggest bear bars formed in 13-16 GMT Interval. After that, lot of dojis shows possible support for bulls. BUY with stop loss below entry bar and TP 1:1. Buy additional position after Interval broke UP. After breakout Close BUY position, because huge bear bar shows possible Bull Traps. Sell at the High with Stop loss above entry bar and TP 2:1, because higher odds that there is the highest point for the rest of the day.

Next day small volumes at the market, small waves with no clear direction. From first look after huge bear Candle (marked) bulls hold the bottom. From NY open bulls try to take control. Big spiked bear bars show Bullish pressure. HL formed and after breakout good signal to BUY. Nice breakout. Sometimes the biggest breakouts or reversals start from small accumulation at the bottom or top.

Bears try to take control and lower the price back. Near the bottom of accumulation zone possibilities are more in Bullish side. Need to wait for confirmation in Interval Price action for make decision. Since NY OPEN Bulls try to take over control from bears. Near Interval Close time you can see Bull candle with big spike from the TOP. After that signal bar shows possible Sell signal with stop loss above the Interval and Take profit no less than 1:1.

Bulls hold at the bottom of the Interval and formed HL.

Next day bears pushes price lower from the top of Interval. Bulls didn't take control. Bearish wave next day – bears attempt to take control. Bottom holds. Big Bulls breakout from NY open. What tells us price action about this breakout? After candle with Big Bull Body, market stopped. Strong bear pressure from the top. Bears try to reverse the market. Market formed high, lots of bull bars with spikes from the top try to form HH. Little bit HH, but candle with Big spike from the top. After Interval CLOSE time, signal bar occurs and entry bar for going to SELL:

Sell high with Stop Loss above the top of the Interval. If the price will stop out, possible go to BUY. Order successful took profit. Next day as you can see interval sows bullish strength. Sell at the high after SIGNAL bar forms. Small stop loss, try to take 2:1. After the price reach 1:1, move stop loss to breakeven.

Some time after Interval Close time, the price breaks the HIGH of Interval. BUY, stop loss below the previous LOW.

Next day the NY open with downside movement. Huge bear bar and after it Signal bar for BUY. Stop loss below signal bar, take profit no less than 1:1. After few big bull bars, bear bar that could warn us about false Entry. 4 consecutive bear bars and Interval Closed. First M15 candle after the CLOSE Strong Signal Bar for LONG positions. BUY with stop loss below the lowest point of Interval. Possible close to breakeven.

Next day bulls from the beginning formed HL and HH. NY opens and after BIG bear candle during Interval Time, forms Bullish signal bar. Possible Lowest point for the rest of the day. BUY low with Small Stop loss. After some time the price breaks Interval. Add extra BUY position.

Bear in mind, that no edge will ever make a trader beat the market. For the market is not a beatable object. If trader is able to apply knowledge, will reach his goals. There are a lot of amount of information in charts of all time frames. Trader must get ability to absorb information and take right decisions based on Price Action, Money Management, and Psychological Perspective.

Our actions of yesterday form the thrust of how we think today. The more positive and higher quality actions we take the more positive and correct our minds become.
Be around people and environments that inspire and activate the good parts of you, interpret things in correct ways, set powerful intentions, and take action so your mind feels stronger, more confident and capable.

Why I confirm that this strategy can offer you High Probability Setups?

This method allowed me to analyze lots of information from history and got statistics. I just took historical data and tested that. Results confirmed my opinion about opportunities during the first 3 most volatile market hours and after them. As you can see, there is near 90 percent probability that the highest or the lowest point of the day was formed during the first 3 hours from NY open.

There is statistics in Excel Spreadsheet in my computer. At the last pages of the book you will find link of my personal website, where I will show some free VIDEOS and LIVE examples of trading High Probability INTERVAL strategy.

EURUSD: 10 years statistic. Sessions when during the first NY hours have been formed the Lowest/Highest point for the rest of the day: 2178. In 10 years perspective as you can see that 87,54% times the highest/lowest point were formed at these hours. Average directional price movement after NY open 3 hours 21.4117 points. As you see, it was only 305 sessions when the price moved inside the 3 hours range after Interval CLOSE time.

2178	87,54%	21,4117	305

3.3. Discipline importance

Winners embrace hard work. They love the discipline of it, the trade-off they're making to win. Losers, on the other hand, see it as punishment. And that's the difference. Once you have clearly outlined and identified trading methodology, you must have the discipline to follow the system. If the way you view a price chart and action on it is different from how you did it month ago, then you either have not identified your methodology or you lack of discipline to follow the methodology you have identified. The formula of success is to consistently apply a proven methodology. If Price Action High Probability Interval strategy shows you good probabilities, bear in mind that it is never 100 percent of success. Markets don't have memory, for market it is not important that was your trading results yesterday, today, never. Every trade is unique and you must take control of it and yourself. Don't try to recline, trading is not game. It is serious work and you must understand that the first of all. There is no fast money.

3.4. Test Yourself:

What Price Action tells you after NY open at this chart? It is M15 chart of EUR/USD, but it is not important that financial instrument chart analyze. Better to concentrate on price behavior:

First questions you need to ask yourself: Do this rising bars show me an UPTREND?

If yes, look for BUY opportunities.

No, it is just rising wave in Interval. V shape market phase. It is Bullish wave in Interval. Look for SELL HIGH SETUP during 3 hours from NY open:

What to do now? Look at bigger picture:

The same Chart H1 Chart:

The Chart shows us that bears are in control of the market – the price moves below 20 Exponential Moving Average. Consecutive bear bars in a row, big spikes from the TOP, Strong Bearish pressure:

Come back to M15 chart: What to do next?

At the high of the possible Interval in a downtrend, small doji formed –
that bar means nothing to us. It is not Signal Bar. One Bar after Doji –
possible Signal Bar. Sell signal. Odds in your side. Bear Trend. Sell High
setup is your goal. Also bear in mind that you are at the NY 3 hours
Interval. High Probability that market can form there the highest price for
the rest of the day. SELL after the Signal Bar with stop loss above the high
and Take profit near the Lowest Point or 1:1 ratio. If high probability, 1:1
risk/reward ratio is proper.

What's next? As you see, the market eats up STOP LOSS. What market dictates now? Failed breakout to the upside. Very Nice SIGNAL BAR for SELL. Probability is Higher – time also is in your side. Now it is 14:45 – closer to 16 GMT, higher probability that there is possible TOP for the rest of the day. SELL HIGH. Stop Loss above Signal Bar, take profit 1:1 or near the bottom of wave.

The Odds that it was the highest point for the rest of the day are higher.15:30 GMT – wait for more opportunities to sell. Nice Signal Bar. What to do now - Sell or Wait? Better to wait, because it is near the bottom of the range:

Strong Breakout to the downside: SELL wit stop loss above the signal bar. Take profit at 1:1. The last BAR you see on the chart is at 16 GMT. So you take one loss and two profitable positions during that time. Now it is time to follow price action after INTERVAL CLOSE time.

SELL after the price breaks the low of 13-16 Interval. It is Friday, so better to close positions before FRIDAY close. Many small candles at the end of the day. Close before the weekend. The strategy is created for short time positions.

Summary: Don't forget to ask questions for yourself. If you are near computer from 13 GMT till 16 GMT – look for possible Highest/Lowest points formation for the rest of day. Bear in mind to look at the bigger picture – Is this movement a trend or wave in Interval. If in trend, look to BUY/SELL for any reasons. If NOT, BUY LOW, SELL HIGH. Also ask yourself about risk management: What reward/risk ratio do you prefer to use? Try to use no less than 1 REAL risk :1 Profit ratio. Don't forget lesson about how to calculate your take profit based on real risk (not initial risk).

4. WAVE PROJECTIONS. CATCH THE SIZE OF THE NEXT MOVEMENT

Trading business is like a game between two teams – two types of investors. Bears want the market to go down. Bulls want the market to go up. Two sides are often fighting for control of trading territory. Some make millions, while others take loses. Always remember, that we are in environment with high participation, so you need to be prepared technically and emotionally. At the later chapter I will share with you some IDEAS of how important emotional Intelligence is. You must obey the rules that market dictates if you are planning to succeed in trading. If you break them, you are more than penalized - you fail.

The market price is always moving between two magnetic zones – the most important support and resistance level, doesn't matter how strong trend is, the end point will be near the strongest resistance level. The essential concepts of trading are always to set Magnetic zones. If you want to SELL, large players also must SELL at the same point if you want to see price action move in your direction. First of all, BUYERS must close positions and ONLY after that SELLERS will be attracted. Sometimes dominant force shows conservative stance, sometimes more aggressive. Whatever trader does, he will make sure it is in accordance with his personal plan or method. Trading is business, before put capital at risk, traders must determine the possibilities and return.

EUR/GBP Daily Chart: Trending market phase. Bearish price action dominates at the market:

The same chart H4 Chart: Trending market phase. Bearish price action dominates at the market:

H1 Chart: Trending market phase. Bears dominate at the market:

M15 Chart: What market conditions do you see there? Is this rising wave a Trend? It is up wave in Interval. V shape formation. BUY LOW, SELL HIGH setup in that trading conditions. V shape formation means that price action can switch to TR. SELL at the high. Magnetic ZONE for rising micro Trend is at 0.75 level. Traders look for exhaustion of bullish forces.

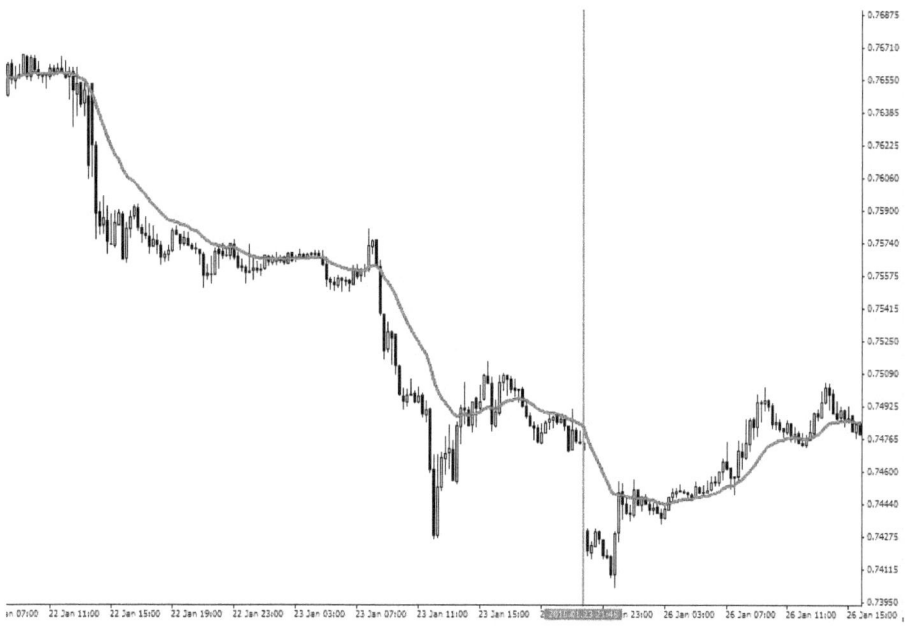

Analyze micro Uptrend: trend starts with Micro Breakout, after that price action switch to channel with small inclination angle. Price action shows us that rising wave is not a TREND, but only wave in TR. Near the level 0.75 traders look for exhaustion and setup with 2:1 reward/risk ratio. Probability more than 50 percent, because SELL signal is in direction of the TREND in bigger picture. Before enter SELL at the market, as a trader you must see exhaustion bar and signal bar. Exhaustion formed when the price reached 0.75 level for the first time. Second time market touched 0.75 level – Double TOP price action formation. Context allows us find for SELL signal. After Signal Bar forms, enter the market with SELL. Reward/Risk ratio must be 2:1 or more. Top of the possible Interval – Magnetic zone:

Wave Projections understanding improves trader's ability to follow price action in possible TR correctly and more accurately. The bottom of possible TR at 0.74, first wave size were 50 pips, measure the same distance and note possible TR TOP. It is at the 0.75 level. Magnetic ZONE is 0.75 level. Don't trade Lows at 0.74, because BUY signal is not familiar with bigger picture TREND (bearish trend).

Bullish wave finished at the 0.75 level. SELL HIGH with 2:1 ratio. What probability for Bears at 0.75 level? Interval market phase, middle zone 0.7450 – 50/50 probability zone, the closer market price goes to 0.75 level, the bigger probability for bears. I do assumptions that near 0.75 chances are near 55 percent. SELL HIGH with 55 percent probability and 2:1 ratio. Don't trade 55 percent probability with 1:1 ratio, only look for places to SELL HIGH with 2:1 ratio or even 1, 5:1.

TR market environment means that both BULLS and BEARS are fighting with each other and try to take over the control. Probability is about 50/50 percent for both sides – that's the reason why waves are usually equal. My favorable trading method in Interval is to measure waves and do projections for determining profit targets or possible price STOP points. First bearish wave from 0.75 top went down to 0.7475. When the price breaks this level, I prefer to do wave projection for the next wave. Possible price STOP point is below 0.7450 level. The closer price goes down to Lower Magnet, the higher probabilities for BULLS.

For the reason that I am not prefer to trade against the bigger Picture Trend, at this place I not try to find Signal for BUY position. It is only my opinion, if Strong signal in Small time frame forms, you can look for BUY signal, but only at the places where 2:1 or more reward/risk possible to reach. Let's look at the picture: V Shape form price action – Two equal waves in TR – Up and DOWN the same amount of pips. At the end of possible bearish wave exhaustion point (the closer price comes down to 0.74, the higher probability for BULLS) wedge formation and strong BULL signal bar. Possibilities for BUY 50/50, but risk reward ratio is more than 2:1 if trader entry at the lowest point and based on small timeframe (M15 or M5).

The price rapidly goes to 0.75 MAGNETIC ZONE. Look for SELL signal Bar. Probabilities are in Bears team side. Nice and clear signal bar has formed and SELL with minimum 2:1 risk/reward ratio. First wave down was till the 0.7465 price level. The closer the price goes to the possible agreement zone (0.7450 – middle TR zone), the greater probabilities to see price move back to 0.75. As long as the price is below 0.75 level (TOP Magnet ZONE), better chances to look for SELL signals at the high with 2:1 ratio. SELL at the high one more time and other times then the price comes to

Magnetic Zone. TR trading requires also follow waves highs and lows. As you see at the picture, bears formed Lower Highs – it is signal that your decision to sell Highs correct.

The price goes down to 0.7435 from 0.75 first time, after some time break that level and the target for BEARS will be based on Interval Projection. Interval high 0.75, Interval middle 0.7465 and possible Bottom 0.7435. Interval as always divided in TWO Zones – Upper zone SELL zone, Lower zone BUY zone. At the middle of Interval Agreement zone, where probability only 50/50 for both sides – BULLS and Bears.

What's next? At the Lower side of the Interval, look for BUY opportunities. BUY signal formed. At the middle of INTERVAL more both sides forces as often. The price rapidly goes to 0.75. Near that level were no SIGNAL to SELL – aggressive Breakout to the upside. Traders must determine – is it successful breakout or failed. As you see at the picture the price goes to

Dainius Silkaitis

new high and after that -correction. Don't BUY at this point, because false breakout probability also high and if the price goes below 0.75 level again, it will be False Breakout Signal and possible SELL below 0.75. As you see, the price went down to 0.75 – resistance becomes support. Don't Buy at this point, because you need to see bigger picture. What this price action means from the bigger picture perspective?

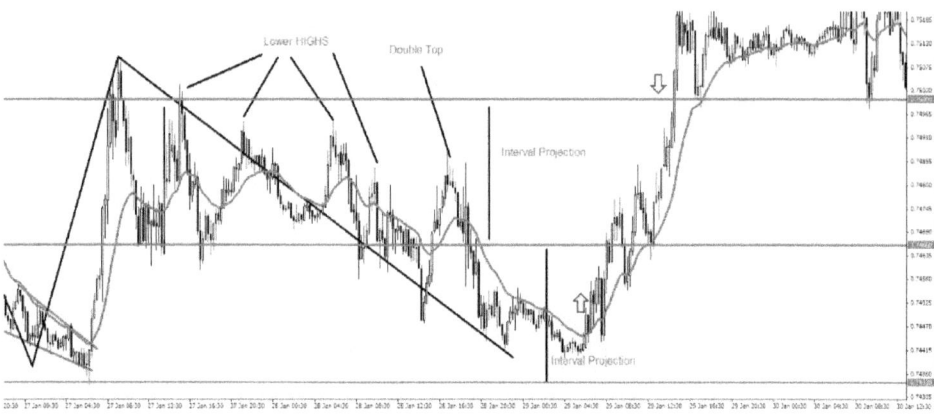

H1 Chart: After the price breaks 0.75 Level, NEW assumptions for probabilities. New Interval. Based on Interval Projections, we set the possible up wave Target and Magnetic ZONE. The closer the prices goes to Magnetic Zone, the greater probabilities for BEARS SELL Signal.

74

What's your behavior should be? Look for Signal Bars near the SELL Zone.
First Sell signal was false, Second – successful. Sell High Setup. How to
determine Signal Bars I will show you in next sections. Below 0.75
Agreement Zone, near 0.74 level possibilities are greater for Bulls. As you
See the market also get chance for BULLS near the bottom of possible
Range. The price went down and broke the 0.74 Level.

Chart from Bigger perspective shows us that Interval movement was
continuation pattern.

SELL ZONE

4.2. **The most important Lesson from Waves Projections Section:**

The hardest part of trading is in Corrective Phase. As long as the market price is at the Trending environment, we always can find good entries and it is not difficult to do that, because one dominant side manages the market. Bulls or Bears are in control. When the price starts corrective phase, always there is possibility to see Range price action. Always ask yourself question about the market phases (more in Section: **Market Development Stages/ Phases).** Corrective Phase specific is that both sides have the same chances (50/50) and for that reason we can do assumptions about agreement zone, Magnetic Zones and INTERVAL projections. Waves in Interval Context usually are equal. Symmetry is specific for the market. Bear in mind that the price usually moves with equal waves. One of the reasons why this works is that traders always try to use 1:1 or 2:1 reward/risk ratio. The market always moves between two magnets – High and Low points that try to magnetize to their own side. For that reason Agreement Zones occurs and reflects consolidation or possible more different side moves. Always don't forget to look at the bigger picture. Understanding of Waves projection and Magnetic Zones help for traders to find the best Reward/Risk trading opportunities.

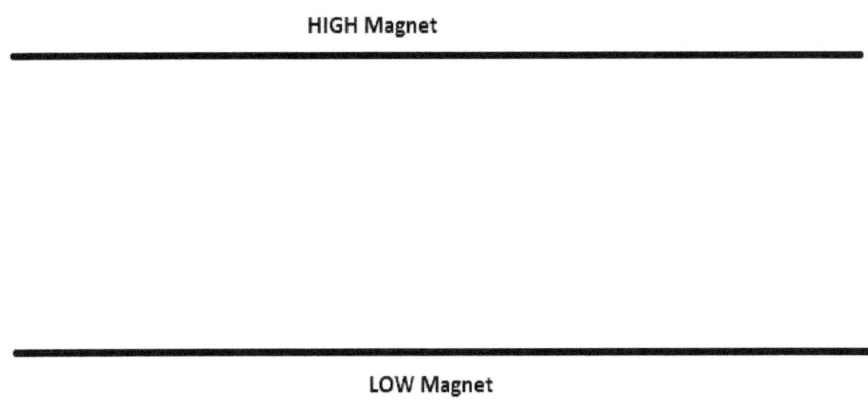

Then the price breaks the Highest Magnet, it becomes Agreement Zone and probability in that zone 50/50 for Bulls and bears. Never try catch up the market. If the price breaks High Magnet, It becomes Agreement Zone of the bigger picture, so there is greater chances wait for correction and BUY on the LOWS at the smaller timeframe.

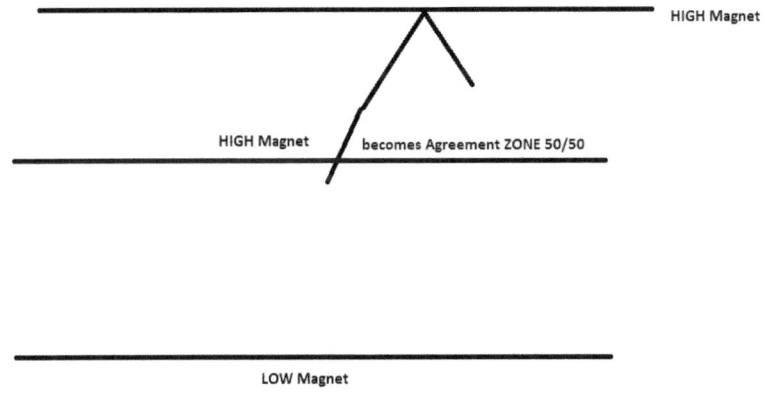

EURUSD Monthly Chart: After 2008 year crash, EUR/USD bounced back to the previous TOP. V shape price action movement means that we are in an Interval phase. Sell High, BUY at the Low, Sell at the TOP, BUY at the LOW. Two sided movement. Don't BUY at the middle zone. Possible Sell exhaustion is near the LOW of wide channel.

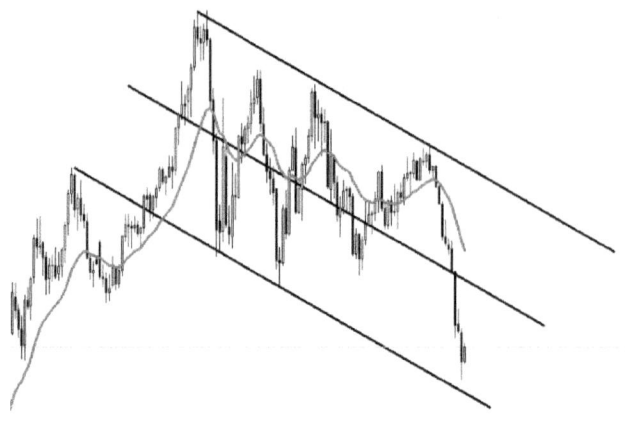

The Same Chart Weekly: Smaller picture, but we can see Two Magnetic Zones and Agreement zone.

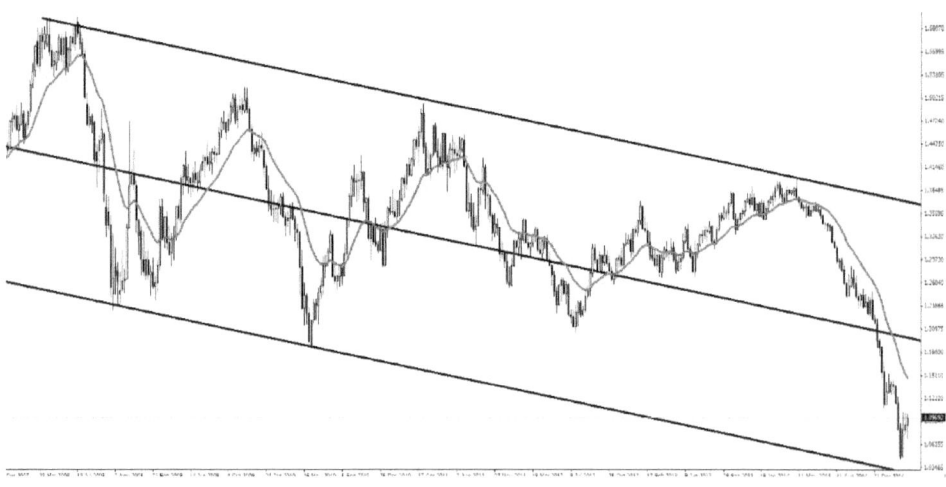

EURUSD Daily Chart. SELL High FROM the Magnet HIGH: The price went down to 1.35 from 1.4. 500 pips wave formed V shape formation – the price came back the same amount of pips as the size of the previous up wave. I highly recommend you follow correction sizes as wrote in book before. If correction lasts for a long, we lose the trend and can't say that we see clear direction at the market. V Shape formation means, that there are more chances for opposite forces at the market to go with correct reward/risk ratio. The price bounced from LOW zone 1.35 till the middle zone. Up wave from 1.35 till the middle zone is not a trend, so we are looking for SELL High opportunities. Setup will form only when micro uptrend finishes. Possible Sell High zone near 1.40, if you want SELL HIGH signal at the middle of the range zone, better to find it in the smaller time frames. Because in Daily chart at the middle zone chances for BULLS and BEARS are the same, risk reward also the same. So it is not Good idea to SELL at the middle Zone with Stop loss above 1.40 and Take Profit 1.35. Better to find SELL Signal at the smaller time frame and try to catch the possibilities with small risk and bigger reward.

Entry situation at Smaller Timeframe: rising Channel is not a TREND. Find for opportunities to SELL HIGH.

Back to Daily Chart: After Sell HIGH at H4 Chart or smaller time frame signal entry, as a trader you must look for possible profit target. 1st profit target is the same size as it was zone between 1.35-1.37. Middle-Lower Interval wave size is projection for the next bears target if the price after 1.35 breakout. First target 1.3250, second target – approximately 1.30 (1.40-1.35 size = 500 pips, second target after 1.350 breakout = 1,30). Now we see Bear trend – sellers dominate at the market. Only Sell.

After the price breaks 1.30 level to the downside, open up opportunities for wait 3rd target. 3rd target is based on Third Projection (1.40-1.30 = 1000

pips. After 1.30 breakout we are waiting for 1000 pips downside movement to 1.21-1.20 zone. Also half point of that distance is possible correction zone). After 1.30 breakout, this level becomes new Agreement zone. Every up wave in the distance between 1.30-1.20 zone is correction and only look for sell Signals and entries.

After 1.20 breakout, the price go down more and the next 4th projection target is 1.000. 1.20 level after breakout becomes new Agreement zone. It is no difference that time frame or financial instrument do you use. Price Action is working on any time frame. People are working on the same principles in all markets – greed and fear emotions are driving the markets every day in all financial instruments. Mostly I use my system for currencies, OIL or SP500 chart, but it is working in all time frames and all financial instruments.

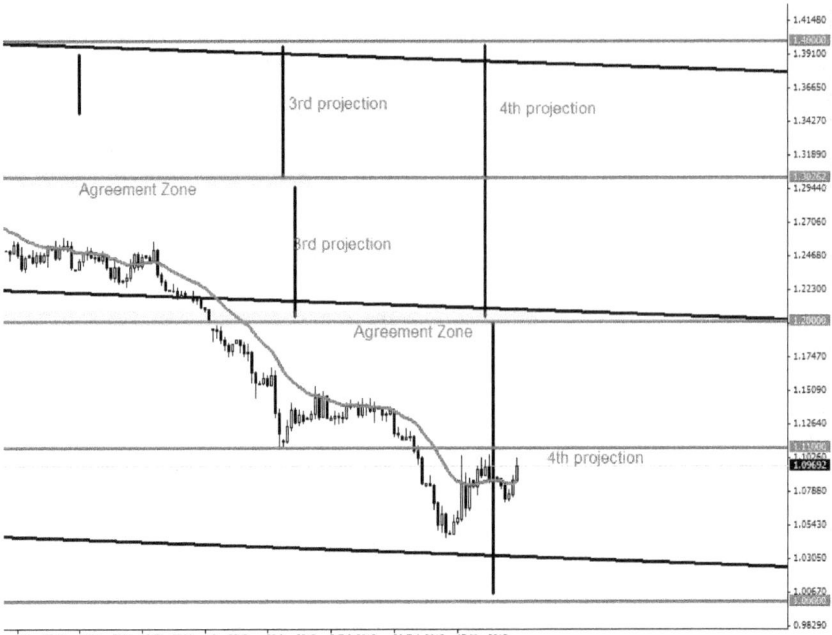

Let's look at other Chart: USDCAD H4 Chart. At this chart you can see and define clear uptrend. There is no question that force dominates at the market. As a trader you need to follow highs and lows in a trend. It is normal and necessary to see HH and HL. Follow Correction sizes. If you can see V shape price movement, work as in Interval – BUY LOW, don't BUY highs, don't try to catch up the price and not rush to the train, that is driving away. BUY at the High only if the Price breaks Interval High. There you can see V shape price action – correction size is too long and traders can lose the trend. BUY Low at the Lowest Point with 2:1 reward/risk ratio or more.

If we do assumption that it is Interval market phase, draw Middle zone.
BUY LOW, don't rush to the train when the price goes up, don't try to BUY
at the HIGHS. SELL High is probable setup – the closer price is going to the
HIGH magnet, the higher probability for bears. I don't recommend to SELL
at these points, because it is setup against the bigger trend. But signal
exists, if you follow smaller time frames you can catch the end of the
micro trends (bullish waves in TR) for SELL entries.

As you can see, the price breaks out the 1.26 level – profit target to 1.28 (
1.24-1.26 zone size = 200 pips, so projection for profit target = 200 pips
after 1.26 breakout).

Bulls and bears enter the market buying or selling in hopes that more bulls or bears will enter after them, giving the market what is called bullish or bearish strength—creating a greater rally or greater dip. If their counterparts step in, the market will begin to move in their direction. Take the bulls, for
example. If you wanted to be a bull, you would enter the market and, if your analysis was right, more bulls would enter and the market would begin to rally and reach new highs, or what is called higher highs. Always check Market phase – context. Does the wave you see the trend or only micro trend. Remember, the market moves always between two Magnets – High Magnet and Low Magnet. Orientation of that should help you to determine the odds of each individual trade and do assumptions that reward/risk ratio fits the best. We should always bear in mind that regardless of our wonderful setups, trades can't be guaranteed. Losses are the costs of our business - sometimes costs are higher, sometimes lower. Therefore, trader can't be euphoric after the winning trade and disappointed after a losing trade – clear signals of misunderstanding of business model. As trader begins to understand that and feel emotions, that are rational and determine realistic goals, the sooner he will be able to see trading as his profession, not as a game or gambling. Discipline is the key for success in all life, there are no less importance of that.

This picture perfectly explains how the price is moving in two magnetic Zones and that emotions feel traders on that. If you want to be in 5 percent successful traders club, you need to think differently and determine Magnetic Zones at the charts. It is not important that financial instrument or time frame, the price is always moving in that way.

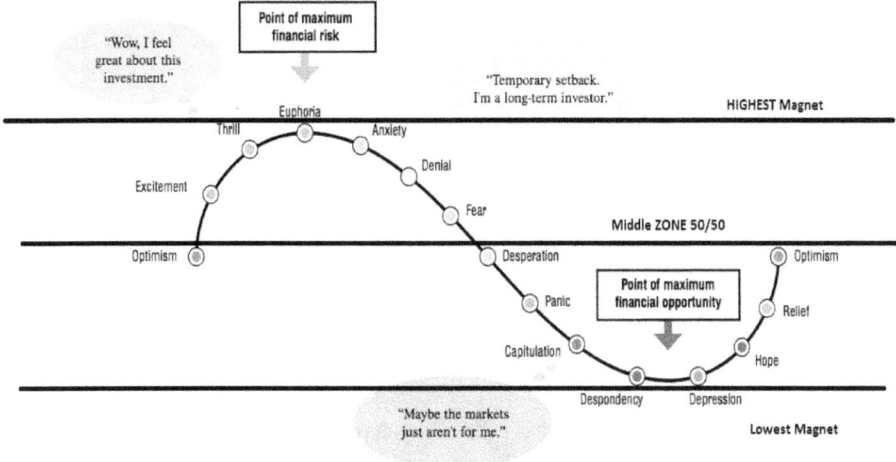

4.3. TEST YOURSELF:

Back to the start of this section and begin to read one more time carefully. Open the chart in real time and try to determine your probabilities, money management rules and possible setup zones on the chart. Also see the picture from psychological perspective. Bear in mind – always look forward. Never try to analyze past or history of the charts. It is one of trader's addictions. Why? As a trader and mentor, who educated a lot of traders, whose sat next to me in my trading courses I never try to analyze past charts, historical charts a lot for one simple reason – in historical charts we tend to see only the places where we were wrong and try to change something in our trading plan, because in one or other places system has not delivered the ,,fruit''. That's one of the thinking differences between successful traders and the rest crowd. Crowd always try to find Holy Grail and system, that can provide high probability – near 100 percent. Successful traders understand that it is not important and enjoy their 55-60 percent probabilities. So if professional trader lost at one place, second time he will do the same at the same situation. Because for him is important to understand market price behavior – price action dictates decisions. Every moment at the market is unique, but if you have good probability and good reward/risk – it is your time to go to the market. For experts setups always look normally. My advice to you: read all my book sections and try to use information in real time. Your workouts must be in real time, don't work a lot with the past, because it is easy to predict when you see that's happened after. Better to analyze left side of the existing chart for determining market phase, market behavior and determine your actions sequences – price action moving scenarios and what you can expect from them. Always ask questions and talk with yourself. The market price is your boss, you must listen to him.

5. BULLS AND BEARS DOMINATION

Bulls and bears keep track of all the previous highs and lows, no matter how far back they go. When bulls achieve a new high—higher than the previous high—they take profits and after that the market pulls back. Conversely, the bears are trying to take profits by taking the market lower and making lower lows. When the bears make a lower low, lower than a previous low, they take profits which is followed by a pullback.

Bear and Bull candles can show us power of dominant force – is it for a long or higher probability to wait for capitulation. As a trader, you should follow price action and determine who controls the market. Always try to view at the market from different perspective. I will show you how to determine when the odds are more in favor of bears/bulls. Trading forces are as politics – when one party wins the majority in parliament, opposite try to take over control earlier than next elections begins.

In my price action method, every day I am looking for market condition – is the market trending or consolidating? Who dominates the market?

At the picture there are a lot of signs that BEARS dominate – more bears bars than bulls, Lower Highs and Lower Lows, every bulls attempt to form correction or new trend bears stop and push price lower. As you see from the picture, there are more bear bars than bulls and that's the reason why we see downtrend. GAP bars also forms, consecutive bear bars without bigger corrections, big tails from the top shows clear BEARS domination.

What does it mean GAP bar?

BULLS domination price action: more bull bars, consecutive bull bars, every time bears try to take over control, Bulls give price back to their control. GAP bars, big tails from the bottom – also signals that BULLS dominate at the market. Also one rule that can help you to save money at the market – if the price moves above 20 EMA, don't SELL, if below 20 EMA - don't BUY. This rule I recommend to use for novice traders more, because experts and more experienced can find good setups for BUY below 20EMA or SELL above.

Who dominates the market? There is no question – Bulls dominate the market. Every time bears attempt to take over control, BULLS back the price to their side. The price nicely moves above 20 EMA. What market phase do you see? No question – ONLY BUY till the places where Bears takes over control/domination.

Trend can go long way till the point of reversal. Remember – near 90percent attempts to reverse the trend fails. Experienced price action professional never tries to reverse the trend –they understand large inertia of the market. It is the same as turn around the train. The market is like locomotive - if it drives fast, the driver can't turn around it quickly. First of all, he must stop the locomotive and then turn around. The same are with the markets – before we will see strong reversal, the price can go long way and move fast to the Upside/Downside. Every time the price goes down in an Uptrend, it is signal, that the car or locomotive turn on the car clutch for the reason to turn the higher gear. One of our goals in TRENDING market environment is to see when the price moves in TOP gear and take profits in time. But don't try to reverse the chart! Before reversal, the price as the car must slow down and try to do turn around. When the price chart is in Interval or Range, both forces try to take over control or domination of the market. In other words, they are trying to break the Interval to their side. For the reason that the odds are equal in Range or Interval, there are too many failed breakouts. But the market gets opportunity for traders to anticipate breakout direction earlier and after breakout to go the market at early stage. What force is stronger?

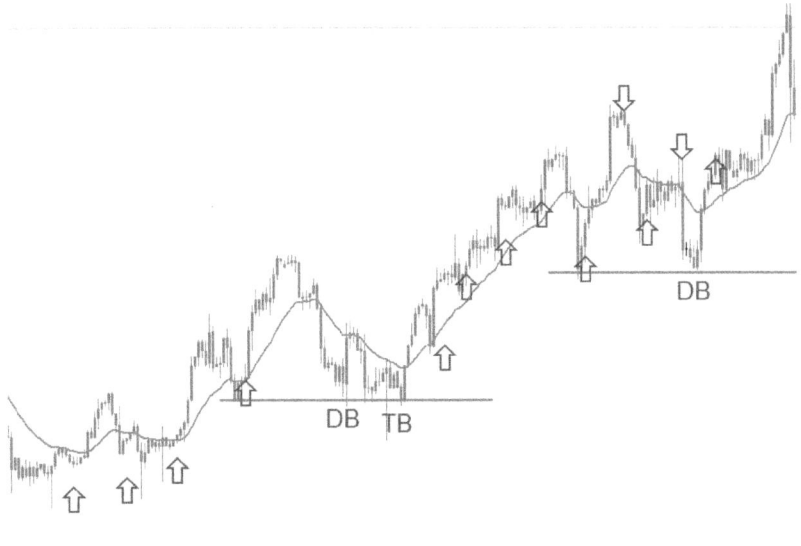

5.2. Who dominates at the chart?

First of all, the market forms HH and Higher Lows. Every time the price attempt to form lower low – Bulls stop the price at the Double Bottom – V shape price action allow us to think about interval and do projections. BUY at the LOWS, BUY when the market forms new Highs, BUY for every reasons. Probabilities are in your favor. Do assumptions that the odds are near 60 percent. Obvious BULLS power at the chart. ONLY BUY.

Let's see at the Breakout market phase (strong BULLS trend) from psychological perspective. High probability for going LONG. Novice traders are willing to wait for a bigger correction. When the probability is greater, the risk is always greater. Why not BUY at the highest point? BUY, but with small position if wider stop loss is needed. After correction you can look for an additional position to BUY with small STOP LOSS. Higher probability in trading means 60 percent. There are no an ideal places at the market. 60 percent probability is good, so 1:1 reward/risk ratio in Trending environment is enough. In Trend, always look for positions with 1:1 ratio. Traders can't control the odds, but can control the risk. If wider Stop needed, an expert in that situation will BUY smaller position. When correction finishes, BUY with small STOP LOSS bigger position and 1:1 ratio. Follow price action and if BULLS forces dominate at the market, look for opportunities to BUY. Don't wait for IDEAL places or Holy Grail. Holy Grail doesn't exist. If the market offers for you opportunity, you should BUY with proper risk management rules. The Trend can go LONG way to the upside before reverse. Never forget to see at the bigger picture also.

At this picture Bears own the market, dominate force. Look for SELL opportunities. Don't wait magical setups. SELL HIGH, SELL LOW – bigger or smaller correction use as a SELL opportunity. Every time Bulls try to take over control, Bears back the price down to the LOWS or NEW LOWS. Lower Highs and Lower Lows. Try to predict the size of the next wave by doing projections. Wave Sizes are usually equal (look at the chapter about Waves projections). Setups never look ideal for novice traders. There are always 40 percent or more probability that your decision was incorrect. For experts every setup looks normal, because their business is dependent on following price action, probabilities and capital management.
As a trader, you need to ask yourself for question: What to do now? Determine the dominant force, if consider what to do – place orders only in direction of the trend. Follow price action and dominant force. Remember capital management rules.

What to do now? Now please read one more time section about DOMINANT forces and open chart of any financial instrument, no difference that time frame. Ask yourself: what are dominant forces at this time? How much trends do you see? If you can clearly recognize the dominant force, follow price action and go with the market. If you can't determine clear dominant force, that's the signal you are in RANGE or Interval. If you are in an Up wave of Interval, look for BUY lows, if the price is near the high of RANGE, look for the place where BULLS give away control for BEARS. At this market phase don't try to follow one force. Opportunities are the same for both forces. You should neither set yourself a certain number of pips or a percentage gain per day or week, but rather that you should seek to maximize the amount of opportunity that the market present to you within any given time period so that you can achieve your best possible returns. The best advice I can get you as you look for trading opportunity is to start your search by asking the question: ,,Do I see a pattern I recognize?'' If there is no clear trend, it means you are in Range (Interval) environment. If clear bulls/bears trend – plan your decisions based on that. Only look for BUY opportunities at the markets and don't look for ideal places – the most important correct reward/risk ratio. Possibilities are in your favor:

Clear Bear Trend: Chances of lower prices increases. Follow the price action. Every candle that market creates gets opportunity to go Short for any reason. Every Bulls attempt to take over control fail. Don't try to reverse the market.

Bulls dominate at the market. Clear dominant force. Why not BUY at the HIGH? BUY for any reason and no difference that price. Higher risk is needed (wider Stop Loss), place smaller position, if the market present you opportunity to BUY at the lower price in a strong Trend – that I call an ideal place. The odds are in your favor in Strong Trend, so you no need to look for the best prices. Follow price action, because all big players bid up and don't look for ideal prices. We BUY not price, we BUY direction.

Bears try to take over control in RANGE (INTERVAL): Two sided price action. The same length bulls and bears waves. Bulls objective to establish Higher Lows, but as long as 1.7175 is not broken, equal chances for both sides. Never try to catch up the price in Range (Interval). Every Up wave is micro Trend and don't BUY Highs as in a Strong Trend. Sell Highs, BUY at the LOWS. As you see at the picture, every time bulls attempt to start aggressive move up, bears suspend them. Take a look at the chart you follow from Bears and Bulls perspective. At this sample chart Bulls hold in Higher Lows, but Bears hold in Lower highs. Who take over control? Bears took control – SELL, Sell Highs to new Lows.

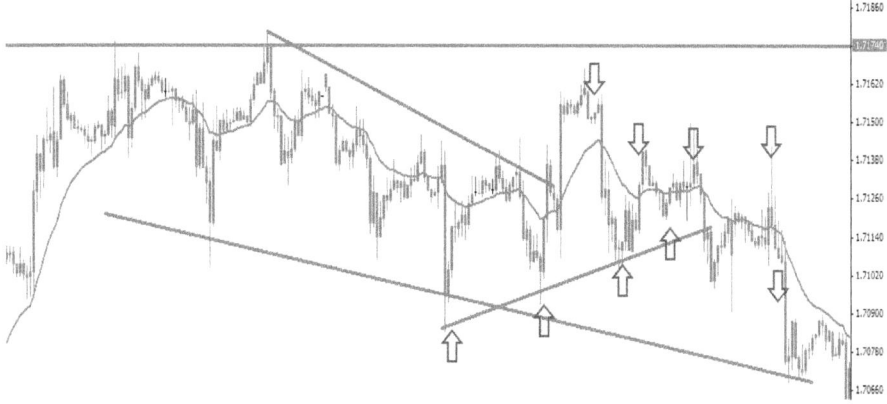

5.3. Interval market Phase:

Bulls intention – form higher LOWS or Double Bottoms and don't succumb to the Bears. Price Action in Range (Interval) allow us to prepare and predict breakout direction. At this Interval Bulls one time tried to break the Interval (HH), after that Double Bottom. Who controls the Interval? Clear Bulls. After some time real Breakout:

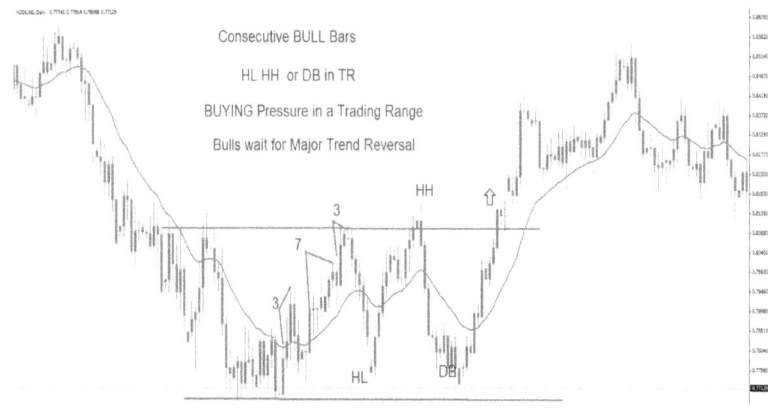

At this chart you can see Bulls domination. At the end of downtrend – last Bear candle is one of the biggest in all trend. It is signal of potential exhaustion. Bulls formed HH, Bears came back and market formed LL, after that LH, but Bulls hold HL and took control.

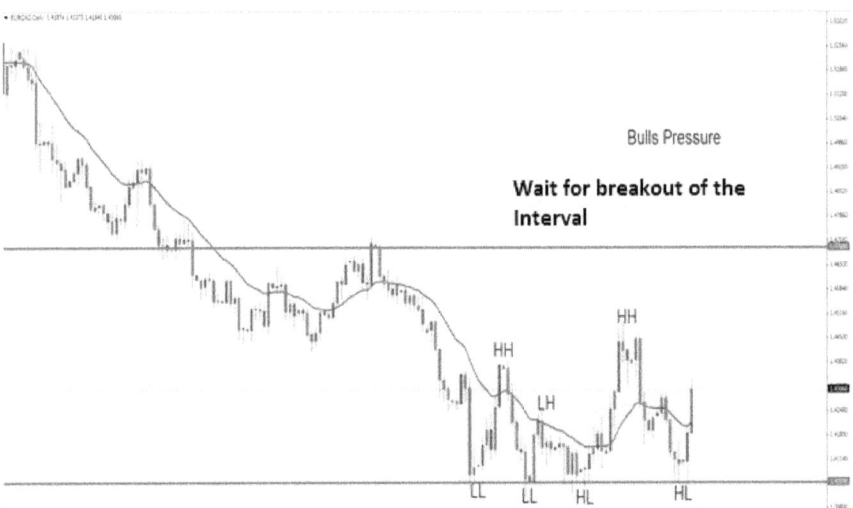

The same chart on smaller timeframe: Market phase Interval. BUY from LOWS, SELL from HIGHS. Two sided price action. BUY only at the places where 2:1 reward/risk ratio possible. Price Action in Interval can prepare us for BULLS or BEARS breakout. At this chart you can see how BULLS try to take over control at the market:

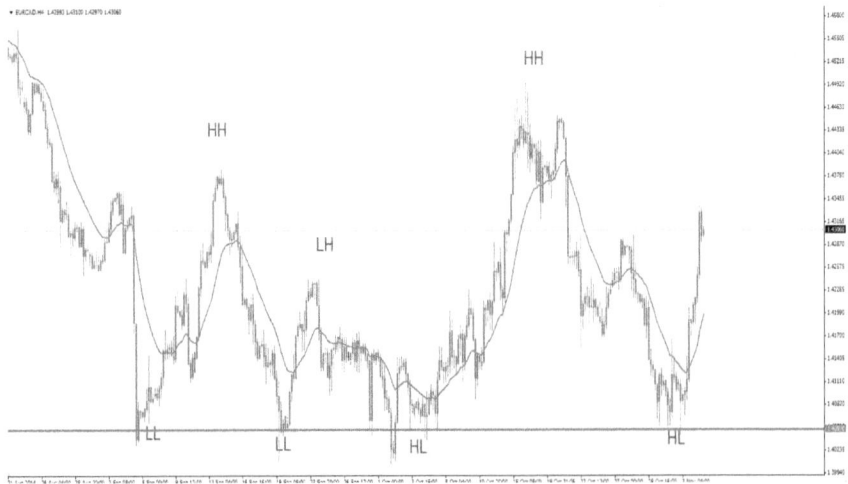

Smaller time frame: Wave down was a micro trend. Traders look for BUY opportunities near the Magnetic support zone. At the bottom we must wait for confirmation signals of BULLS control – HL, HH and DB – signal if potential BULLS domination at the market.

We should ask ourselves at least the following question: do the forces supporting the position appear strong enough to sufficiently counter the forces against it in order to justify the payment of the spread. The more we can answer that affirmatively, the better the odds will be.

Trader should ask ourselves also about the strength of the breakout. Do bulls breakout strong or weak? It is weak breakout, because it forms micro Trend in Interval (Range). Sell at the High of the Interval. Possibilities 50 percent, reward/risk ratio must be no less than 2:1.

Market never move with high degree of inclination angle for a long time. Because there is always two sides – bears and bulls. There are opportunities for both of them every second. The Trend usually starts with high degree inclination angle breakout, after some time corrections become more and more aggressively. That mean bears attempt to reverse the trend. More than 70 percent attempts to reverse the trend fails. Market goes to channels, after that transform to Interval. It is natural pause of the TREND. To determine the market phase correctly is crucial for traders. It helps to trade better and avoid a lot of mistakes. Bulls channel with increasing bears power means possible transformation to Interval. Bears channel with increasing bulls power means possible transformation to Interval.

Strong Bulls breakout, strong Bulls Channel with increasing bears power and transformation of Interval. Never try to catch up the price after the price breaks the channel down. Ask yourself: does this downside movement is a trend? It is not a trend, it is wave in Interval. BUY LOW at the end of the Bear micro Trend. Don't try to sell High, it is counter trend signal, look for BUY opportunities at the LOWS of Interval. Always think about context – where are you from bigger timeframe perspective.

Analyze this chart at the same manner:

More selling power and pressure in Bulls Interval. Only look for BUY opportunities at the LOWS – follow the Lows of the Interval – HL, HL, HL and Breakout. Bulls continue dominate at the market.

Is this a BULL trend or Strong Breakout phase? BUY after breakout only in smaller time frames and look for selling opportunities at the HIGH with 2:1 or more.

No edge will ever make a trader beat the market. The market is not a beatable object. Price Action dictate all conditions at the market. Trader must invest in proper education like all entrepreneurs – invest in their business and education.

6. SIGNAL BARS, ENTRY BARS

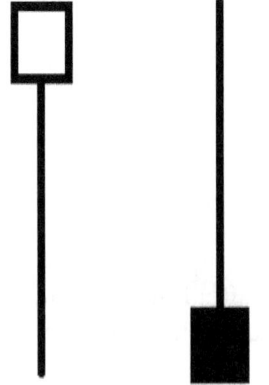

One of the most important things for trader is to recognize the Signal and Entry bars. In this chapter I will show you how I use signal bars to help filter trade entries. The better price we enter the market, the better profit opportunities open behind us. My price action method is to follow every candle in the market and try not to miss good entries. I recommend never calculate the money, but focus on the market opportunities, entries and capital management the most.

Before entry to the market trader must see potential of the situation and clear signal candle. Every time the market is in the Interval, Breakout, and Channel phase. Ask yourself: is this price movement a trend or Interval? Answer to this question helps you to do assumptions. If it is a trend, you can do assumptions that it is about 55-60 percent odds of success. 1:1 Reward/Risk ratio is proper capital management on this phase. If it is only the wave inside the Interval, assumption that only 45-50 percent chances of success. BUY at the LOW, SELL at the HIGH of the Interval. Proper reward must be 2 times bigger than the risk. The middle of the Interval – 50/50 zone. The closer the price near the TOP, the greater the chances for Bears, the closer the price near the bottom, the greater the chances for BULLS.

Every market phase provides us different conditions and rules to trade the market. A signal bar is simply a single candlestick or bar within a pattern that signals to us as traders that a trade entry is likely setting up. A signal bar must complete and close before it can be a signal bar, so this part is really important. Once your signal bar has completed and closed, the trade will not actually trigger unless there is a break or movement of prices below our signal bar if looking for a short entry. So you must wait and filter out the best trades, don't try to trigger position before signal bar formation. I've also seen many bars that appears as if they are going to set up to be great signal bars, only to see those bars change rapidly just before they close and then not turn out to be good signal bar, so these are all the reasons why it is better never guess about a signal bar and attempt to enter early. By guessing and entering early, we become gamblers. And it is addiction. Try to avoid all addictions and determine your personal character traits that can stop your perfection. If you want to be profitable trader, take only trades where the odds are stacked in your favor, follow entry rules and be strict about them.

If we are looking for BUY or SELL opportunities, we need to wait for a Trend Bar or a reversal type bar that closes in the direction of our trade entry. Preferably our signal bar will close on or very close to the high of the candle if we are looking to BUY, and at a very close to the flows of the candle if we are looking for SELL opportunities. The price action before signal bar formation also shows additional strength in our desired entry direction, as it takes Buying pressure to break above a previous bar, or selling pressure to break below a previous bar. Trading for a living, like anything worth learning and that pays very well, takes time, effort and hard work, which most people are not willing to commit.

I will show you Signal Bar setups that work the best. Some setups work very well in trending price action environment, while others traders recognize hardly in Interval environment. Bear in mind, that signal Bar quality depends on context.

At this picture you can see Strong Bear Trend. The price moves below 20 EMA, consecutive bear bars in a row, every bulls attempt to reverse fail. Never try to catch the reversal – usually they fail. Only look for reversal signal bars near the Magnetic zones, where could be potential exhaustion. There you can see strong Bear Trend. Every Bull bars sequence – micro trends and we are looking SELL HIGH opportunities – Signal Bars at the High of Micro Trend.

Context dictates for us look for SELL opportunities. And we must listen the price action that dictates conditions every minute/day/week/month. Every Bulls attempt fails after Signal Bar closes as a Bear bar – tail from the top, closes near the lowest price of the period. That means as a Signal BAR. Entry the market only then the price goes below Signal BAR lowest price. If you can't wait, you have gambling addiction. Try to remove that personal trait from your routine:

At this picture you can see supportive context for BUY opportunities. Don't look for SELL opportunities even STRONG signal bar forms. As you can see, usually in a strong trend after Reversal Bar signal formation, the price goes down small distance, rarely reach 2:1 target for sellers. Usually Reversal Signal bars in a Strong Trend means not signal, but Bear traps. BUY with 55-60 percent probability in a clear Trend and use 1:1 reward/risk ratio.

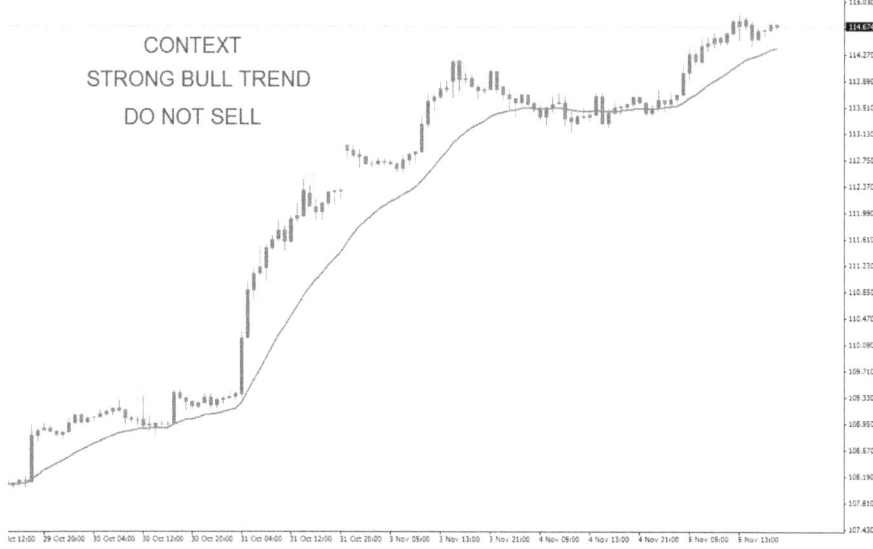

SIGNAL BAR and Entry. One important rule – Doji bar never can be as a signal BAR. Doji bars only mean equalization of bears and bulls forces, consolidation. After Signal Bar with Full bear/Bull body forms, you must wait for breakout of signal BAR extreme for going LONG/SHORT.

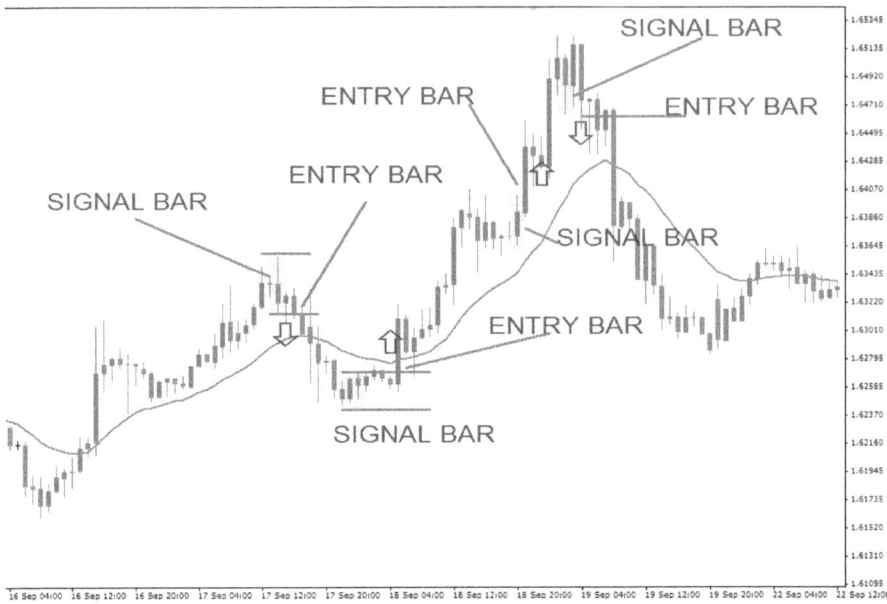

Reversal Bars appearance:

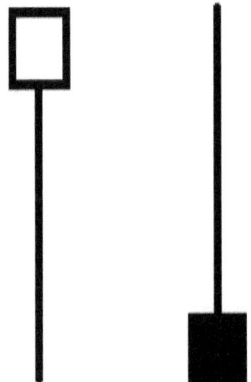

Signal BAR appearance is like normal BULL/BEAR bar.

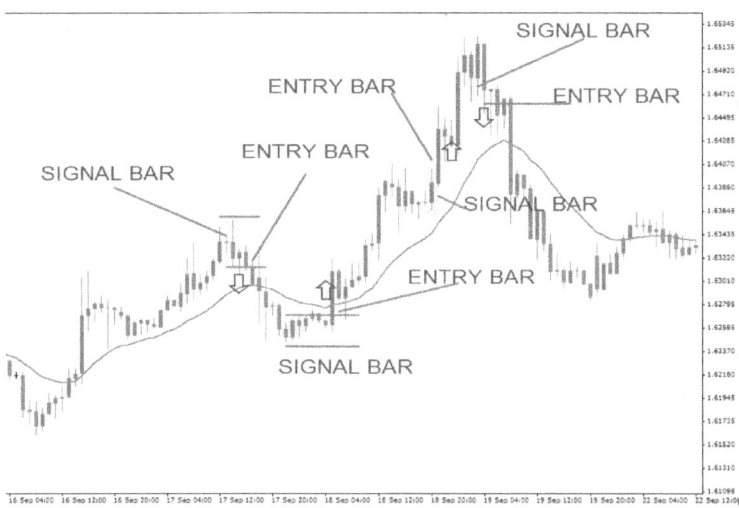

First goal for you as a trader is ability to read price charts correctly and understand market participants behavior that is based on two emotions: fear and greed. Understand setups by themselves have very little meaning. Only if context or market environment is favorable, pressure of price from one side larger than from other side. Otherwise, you see a lot of Reversal Bars in every wave and they fail then you enter the trade. In a Strong Trend, every signal bar even weak will get results for trader who follows the trend.

I never recommend to trigger to the market after one Reversal Bar, better wait for 2-3 bars reversal formation. Don't try to catch up reversal early, because if trend reverses strong, you will have opportunity to go to the market little bit later and earn money from that. Every Reversal Signal Bar shows for us possible reversal opportunities, but one bar it is not enough. Better wait for 2-3 bars formation, not necessarily in a row. These bars tandem form large 1 signal Bar in a larger time frame.

6.2. 2 bars Reversal Signal

The first signal that warns us about possible bull attempts to reverse is Bear Bar with Big Tail from the Low. Is this a signal Bar for Bulls? Not, because close as a Bear bar. Next Bar Inside bar, but has full bull body and closes at the high of the period. Then the price breaks the extreme of that bull bar, possibilities to go LONG with conditionally small Stop Below

Signal Bar. Price Aggressively goes up and take Bulls profits. Bulls dominate at the market – the price moves above 20 EMA. Obvious Bulls Strength. Bearish waves – corrections, because every bear bar is overlapped by BULLS. How to know where is possible correction end point? The best way I use – wait for the biggest bear bars in a micro trend. It wars us about possible exhaustion of bears. After that bar I recommend to wait for a BIG BULL bar which closes near the high. As you see, every time big bear bar forms, Bulls try to regain control of the market and signal Bar forms. Perfect BUY opportunities for traders, who are always looking and following the trend. In Strong Trend environment better don't look for reversals – most attempts will fail. From my personal experience, near 80 percent reversals are false signals. If you ask yourself BUY or SELL, better find opportunities in direction of Trend. Always premise yourself, that 55-60 percent chances of success when open order in direction of TREND.

If the Context is not supportive for one sided price movement, you are in Interval (Range). Better always look for opportunities BUY LOWS and SELL at the Highs, at the middle of Interval there is only opportunities for scalping, but it need more experience. You must understand, that more than 50 percent of time the price moves in Intervals and that means two sided movement. There is only temporary Bulls/Bears control at the market. After breakout of the Interval, there is also probability that it can be false breakout. At this chart you can see breakout of the Interval, correction and possible BUY signal. After small upside movement, Bears come back and the price goes below Interval. False breakout signal. Close BUY position and SELL immediately. Sell High with opportunity to get 2:1 ratio.

At this situation, an environment or context is not supportive for BULLS at the HIGH, because nice Bulls signal Bar was formed at the HIGH of interval. If you analyze price action before, better recognize that market is in Interval. First of all was breakout, after that market formed channel. Channel means weaker trend. More opposite forces appear. Breakout of the channel doesn't mean that the market changes direction. Channels usually transform to Intervals. BUY at the LOWS when Bears micro trend finishes. BUY at the LOWS, don't look for BUY at the highs even nice or Ideal signal bar forms. BUY LOWS better decision, which can get you possibility to trade with 2:1 or more.

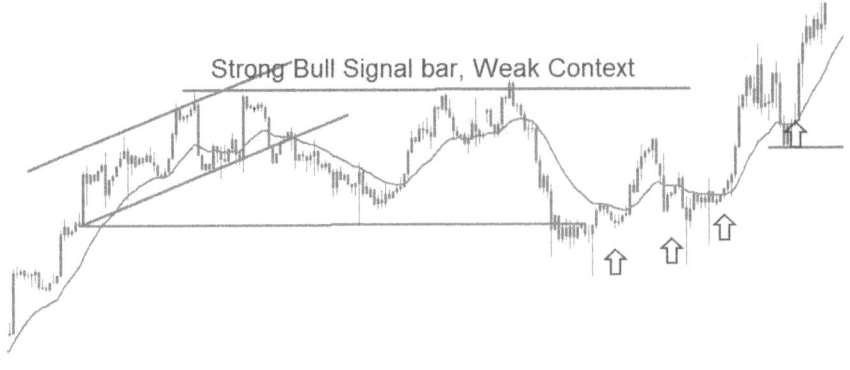

At this Chart you can see strong Bear Trend. An environment is supportive for one sided trading – Bears dominate the market. Follow them and try to get from the market the most that situation can offer you. But it is weak environment for BULLS even Strong Signal Bars or Reversal Pin bars form. There is example of nice Signal reversal bars, but context is not supportive for BUY orders. I recommend you to wait for Bull traps in these situations and SELL when Bulls experience losses from BUY orders.

If you learn to understand price movements and what the chart is telling you, then you can learn to predict, with a high probability, where prices are going, at least in the short term. The ability can make you very successful financially, but do not expect it to be quickly or easily. You must be dedicated and you must pay your dues in time, frustrations and simply staying focused and not giving up or rushing to trade live with your real funds. Day trading is not a get rich quick program. If you approach it like most people whose are gambling in the market, I guarantee that you will fail. It takes time, hard work, dedication and experience. Discipline is your key to successful trading.

Sometimes the chart gives us little information. What to do if you have little information or uncertain environment? There you can see V shape price movement. 3 Strong Bear bars in a row, at the bottom of possible Interval Strong BULL reversal Bar forms. Is it time to BUY? Better wait for more information. Next bar Doji says nothing important to you. Next Bull candle confirm possible BULLS entry. If the price breaks the extreme of that bulls bar, possible BUY entry point. Be patient and wait or place BUY STOP order. If that not happens, don't BUY. Try to avoid premature decisions.

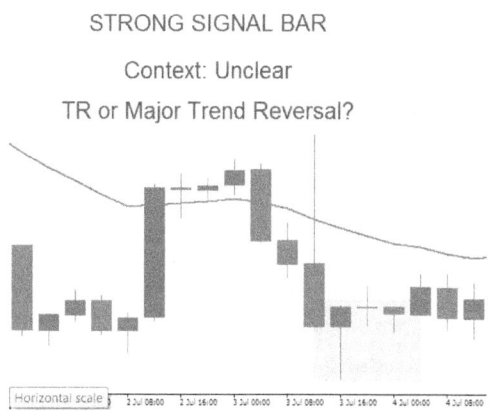

STRONG SIGNAL BAR

Context: Unclear

TR or Major Trend Reversal?

At this chart you can see good environment – Context for looking Short positions. At the High of V shape movement (interval), you can see bars with huge tails from the TOP. But body of candles are bullish. Wait for candle with clear Bear body and then SELL with 2:1 ratio.

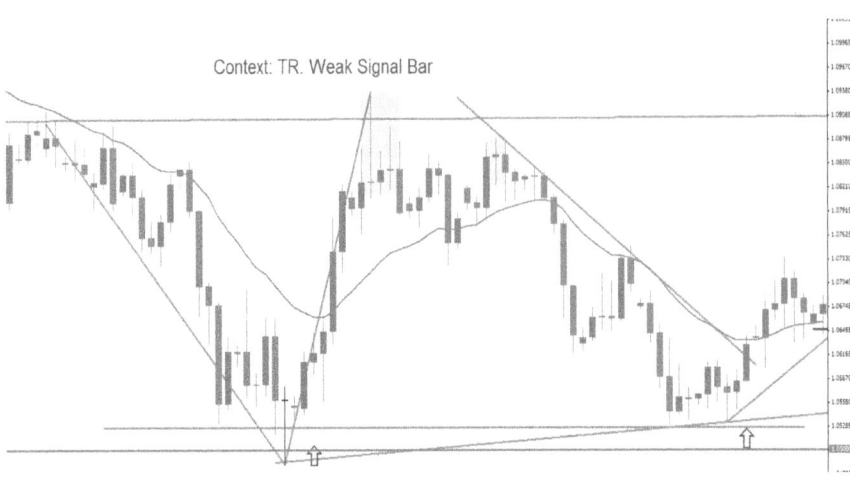

Context: TR. Weak Signal Bar

Trading against the dominant trend always is more risky way to earn money. The odds are not in your favor, you need to find signal, which can offer you 2:1 or better ratio. At this chart after long term bears domination in the market, expanded Interval was formed. It signals for us that Bulls become more aggressive, they try to take over control in the market. At the Low of Interval, it was attempt to breakout Interval and continue Bears domination. After breakout bar never go to the market immediately, because a lot of attempts to break the Interval fail. After breakout Strong signal Bar was formed. Good entry for BUY with small risk and 2 times bigger reward. The odds at this place near about 50 percent, bus good risk reward opportunity pushes traders to capitalize that. Fear can't interfere you – there is never 100 percent probabilities. Loses are normal thing in that business. Only prepared psychologically trader can expect high return in trading. Never try to define how much pips or percent in a month you want to earn. There are a lot of possibilities every day, but there are days that can't provide you good entries. Better to concentrate on your education, risk control, psychology and results will come automatically. Every people has reward center in their brains, and this is the reason why we need results. As I mentioned before, day trading is not a get rich quick program. If you approach it like most people whose are gambling in the market, I guarantee that you will fail. It takes time, hard work, dedication and experience.

This is a Strong Trend. Don't be lured by strong or weak Signal Bars against the direction. There is no reason for going SELL, because you are in clearly defined Bulls Trend.

At this chart Environment are supportive for bears. Context is not good for going LONG, also at the Low Weak Bulls signal bar. Don't BUY at the places like this:

Does this Bullish wave the Trend? It is micro trend, where experienced traders looking for SELL opportunities at the High. At this chart there is no Strong Signal Bar for going SELL. Always better to wait for more information.

Big Bull candle and after it nice signal candle – Full bear body, tail from the TOP, closes near the lowest price. Sell if the price breaks the lowest price of that Signal Bar.

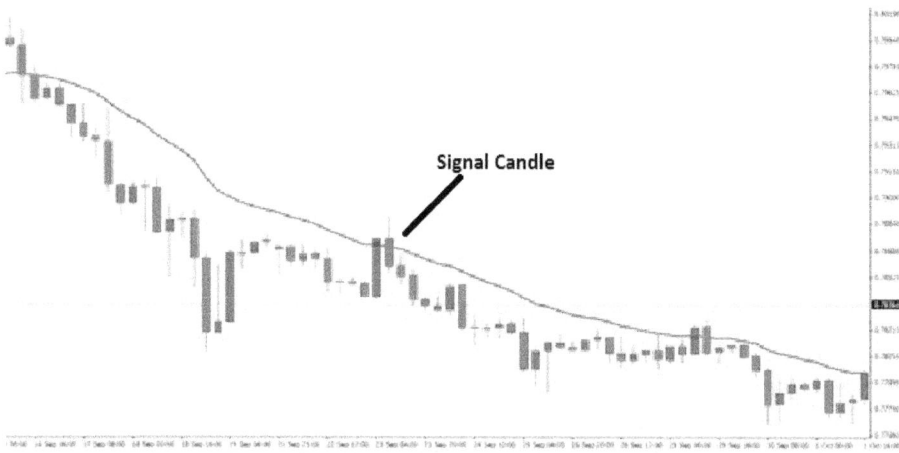

Environment don't support BUY opportunities. Signal Bar at the Low also not strong enough to reverse the Trend. As a trader you need to wait for more information. Two big BULL candles in a row means Strong Bull Breakout. BUY opportunity. Wait for correction – follow price action in corrective phase. Do Bulls have enough Strength to keep the price at the High? As you see from price movement, every bears bar overlapped by Bulls, Tails from the bottoms, at the Lowest point of the Bears micro Trend big candle with big tail from the bottom. This spiked candle shows potential end of the micro trend. Traders wait for BULLS signal bar for going BUY. Remember, if you are trading against the dominant Trend, the odds (only 35-40 percent probability) are not in your favor, so the only thing that can attract you to enter – small risk and bigger reward.

Always look for BUY in this Bull Trend until the price will reach the TOP magnetic ZONE. V shape price movement in the bigger time frame. One of the biggest Bull candles informs us about possible exhaustion. Look for SELL opportunities at the High with 2:1 and greater reward.

Sometimes there is good and supportive environment to look for BUY or SELL opportunities, but weak Signal Bar forms. In these situations you need to wait for stronger Signal Candle. At the High of Interval Bull body candle with large Spikes from both sides. It means consolidation of Bulls and Bears. Wait for strong Bear candle and go Short if the price goes below that candle. Use no less than 2:1 ratio in Interval Trading environment. The same situation occurs at the Low of the Interval. You are looking for BUY opportunities, but need to wait for Signal for entry. First of all at the lowest point bear candle with Big tail from the bottom, after that you need to see clear Bull candle. A lot of candles with spikes from both sides means there is no self-determination. After some time Big body candle. Buy when the price goes above Signal Candle high.

Sell and BUY in micro trend, but remember – the closer the price is near the bottom/TOP of Interval, the greater the chances for Reversal. Try to capitalize all opportunities that market offer.

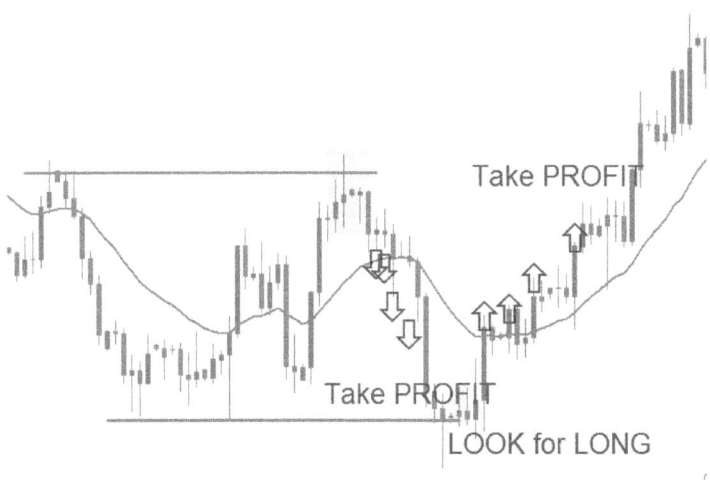

If you can't hit to the trade correctly from the first or second time, don't try to enter the market at the same place third time. Because this manner means that you need to recline. Don't be as a gambler, be professional and follow your rules, follow price action.

Unclear environment/Context. First attempt to Reverse the bear wave fails.

Second Attempt was successful:

If first attempt to BUY fails, look for 2nd entry with 2:1 ratio. Chances when the context is unclear are no more than 50 percent. Why risk with low probability if you can get only 1:1? The main motivation to risk with that LOW probability is better reward/risk ratio. If 2nd attempt fails, don't try to enter the market at the same place for the 3rd time.

The better price we enter the market, the better profit opportunities open behind of us. My price action method is to follow every candle in the market and try not to miss good entries. I recommend never calculate the money, but focus on the market opportunities, entries and capital management the most. If you read this book , you will at least be getting the proper coaching, so then it is only up to you to put in the hard work studying, practicing and honing your skills the way I coach them to be done. Most will lead you to believe that the markets have a great secret or Holy Grail and they can sell you it for a large amount of money. There is no magical secret or Holy Grail that will suddenly make you successful as a day trader. If you want to be in a 5-10 percent of traders that makes money, study charts diligently and remove personal traits or additions that can interfere your way to success. About 50-70 percent of volume is traded by computers – black box trading systems. The biggest benefit of using automated systems is that you remove human error. A major challenge with automated trading is that the markets are dynamic, changing. Trading system developers in Wall Street have the staff and budget to stay on top of changing market environments, where most individual traders do not. As a retail trader you can see that largest financial institutions are doing at the market. Price action is created by all the most important financial institutions, hedge funds, big individual investors, retail traders. There is no better way to trade manually than follow price action. The same as it was then Jessie Livermore traded, the same is now – if don't believe, try to see at the charts form the past – 1930, 1940... What's the difference between them and nowadays charts? The main market movers are the same: fear and greed. And until people nature is that, the same rules will work. Algorithms also work the same. They are based on indicators, news ... But they are created by people, whose behave more irrationally in the markets than rationally. Price action aims at understanding psychology of the market using price action patterns. No one can predict where the price will go the next moment. However, we do have high degree of estimation if we know the structure of anything. Similarly is the case with markets. Price action also helps us as to eliminate a lot of false signals reduce noise.

7. False trend reversals. Traps for Bulls/Bears

One important rule which can help you to save a lot of money is that between 70-80 percent of attempts to reverse the trend fail. So the market a lot of times try to persuade us to trade in bad direction and behave irrationally at the markets, deviate from our trading system or plan. Sometimes for my students I recommend to do one thing: ,,Don't buy till the price is below 20EMA, don't try to sell if the price is above 20EMA." One negative impact from this rule that sometimes can miss better price opportunities, but at the time when trader doesn't have experience, it helps to trade more disciplined.

At this section I will show you how to define False trend reversal signals or Traps for Bulls/ Bears which dominate the market.

First of all, remember, that trader must think before entry about price action, capital management and psychological perspective. Why do you do the trade? What is probability? How do you determine the probability? For me, reliable approach is to know that always, even at the best or ideal places, we have no more than 55-60 percent of success on every trade. That helps me to avoid overconfidence. In other words, if I trade in the direction of the Trend, I do assumption that the odds are in my favor, I have about 55 -65 percent of success, but if the trade is against the trend, the best possibility the market can offer me is 35-40 percent, maybe less. Why risk at the market if possibility is too small? The only reason at these places can be only good reward/risk ratio. Why risk a lot if take profit only with 1:1 ratio? The smallest ratio that would be rational to use in trading against the trend must be no less than 2:1, I personally always use 3:1 ratio in trading against the trend. Think about trading as a business. Every second there are buyers and sellers at the market, supply and demand. Price Action dictates conditions for our trades. Don't try to look for guarantees at the market. If a trader has 90 percent accuracy ratio in the market, his capital management as a rule is poor. Usually his risk is 6 or more times greater than the profit. In trading, our goal is not to be right, our goal is to make the money. Fight with your ego every day in the market. The market doesn't know who you are in real life – every player don't know that will be at the future. If you want to trade with smaller than 1:1 ratio, you must be right 70 percent times. No one professional trader or hedge fund manager aspires that. You goal is to have 50-55 percent accuracy.

The probability depends on the market phase or context. If we are in strong breakout market phase, the odds are greater to work in breakout direction. But at this phase as I wrote in sections before, risk usually are greater, you need wider stop losses. But you can control position size and that's great. The probability is always unknown for us. We can manage the risk.

If you trade against the trend or like that, bear in mind that you are trading setups with low possibilities. So you need to find the places where low risk entries can offer you high reward, because if you trade with 1:1 ratio against the trend (probabilities 35-40 percent), your portfolio goes only down. As I always say for my students, there is no magic at the markets, only knowledge help you to become intelligent trader, investor. You can be the best market analyst in the world, but if you don't have the proper 'mental confluence', you will never make consistent money at the market. Essentially, trading success, like most things in life, is the end result of doing a lot of little things right, consistently.

The market is forming a lot of Traps for Bulls and Bears, especially at the situations when there are attempts to reverse the market.

7.2. How trend reversal develops?

First of all, the price breaks the trend line or strong support/resistance level. Price action warns traders about possibility of trend reversal. A lot of traders get into these traps and are stopped out after some time. What objectives have bears at the downtrend? Their objectives are to form Lower High and Lower Lows at the market. What objectives have Bulls at the uptrend? Their objectives are to form Higher Lows and Higher Highs.

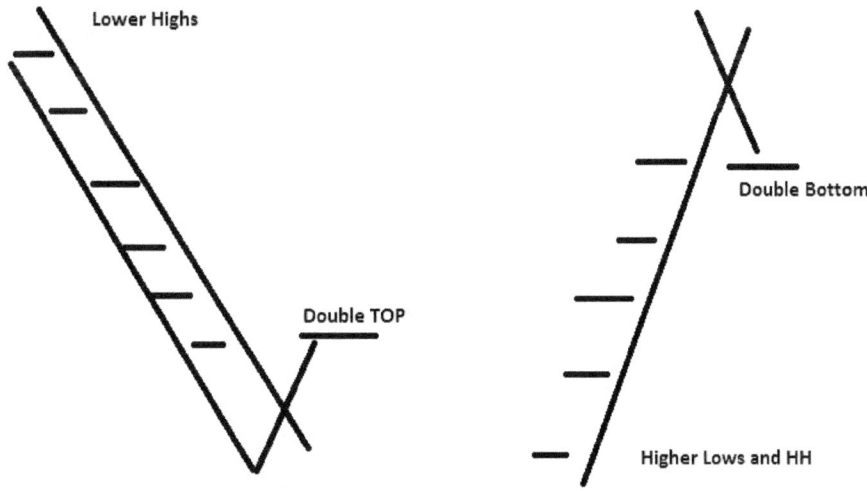

After breakout of the Trend Line or Strong Support/Resistance never try to catch up the market and BUY/SELL in the direction of the breakout. Bear in mind that Bears objective in a downtrend is to form Lower Highs, Double TOPS and LL. They are waiting for opportunities to go for Sell at the better price. So breakout – Bulls attempt to reverse the market attracts more demand for their SHORT positions, brings more liquidity. Institutional investors are waiting for Trap signals, because it provides an opportunity to trade with low risk and greater reward ratio.

The same in uptrend. Bulls dominate at the market, their objective is to create HH, HL or double bottoms. If the price tries to break the trend line or a strong support level, BULLS wait for signal to go LONG in a Double Bottom. Their risk is small, reward 1:1 meet their strategy. The odds are in their favor also.

There is an example of a downtrend. When the price breaks the trend line and 20EMA, bears look for opportunities to sell with 1:1 risk/reward ratio, the odds are in their favor. Double TOP signals. Don't try to catch up the Bulls breakout, because the odds are not in your favor, also greater risk.

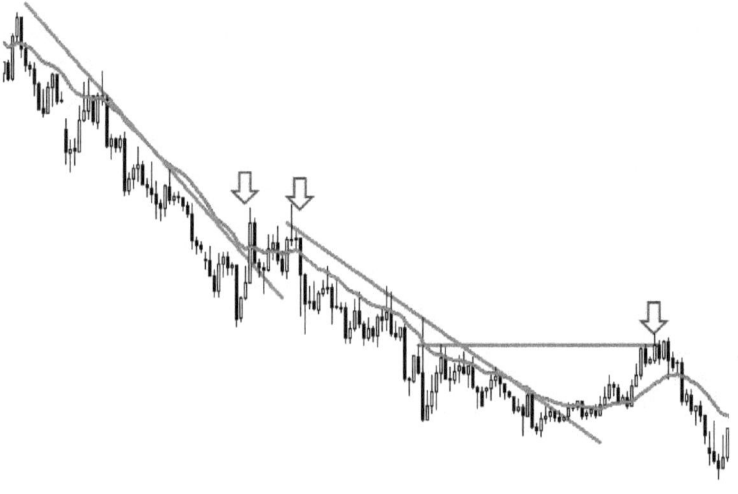

At the BULL Trend the same situation: There are a lot of attempts to reverse the trend or Traps for Bears, whose are waiting for reversal. Every time the price breaks the trend line or previous support, BULLS find for opportunities to BUY at Double Bottom signal with Low risk and reward with no smaller than 1:1. The odds are in their favor.

At this chart Bulls dominate at the market. Bulls spike or breakout phase. The probabilities are in Bulls favor, but as the market goes higher and higher, the risk increases. Don't try to wait for an ideal prices, buy for any reason. You can control the risk and BUY at every place in this market phase. Consecutive BULL bars in a row, Bear candles with spikes from the low, Bear bars overlapped by Bulls. Buy even the price looks high. If wider Stop Loss is needed, BUY with Small position, BUY bigger position then the price retraces. When the price breaks the trend line, follow price action after that. Bear bar – consolidation or overlapping bull bars shows us that Bulls force more powerful at the market. You can't affirm that bears took control from Bulls. For that reason find opportunities to BUY with LOW risk and no less than 1:1 reward ratio. Every time you are looking at the markets, try to view from two different perspectives: Bulls and Bears. Bulls at this chart wait for Double Bottom opportunities, Bears are waiting for Lower high or Double TOP setup from trading against the trend.

Double Bottom

SELL HIGH setup near the TOP. The odds are not in your favor, if SELL only with 2:1 ratio. Better to skip SELL opportunities, despite nice SELL signal forms. Better try to wait for BUY opportunities – HL or Double Bottom Setup. You can First time near the bottom signal bar has formed – BUY signal with 1:1 ratio. After some time bears tried to form lower High, but Bulls hold double bottom and another BUY signal with higher probabilities:

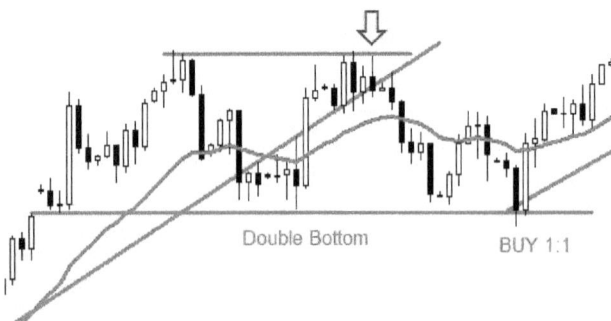

Double Bottom   BUY 1:1

Price action trade signal that's in-line with a strong trend has extra weight behind it and we can even consider the trend itself as a major factor of confluence supporting a particular trade signal. If you get a signal that forms after a retrace to a support or resistance level within a trend, that signal has formed at a high-probability point within that trend, and at that point it definitely has confluence.

Why don't BUY at the highest point? Bulls dominate at the market. Buy for any reason, even Big Stop Loss is needed. Traders can control position size. BUY with small position if wider STOP LOSS is needed. BUY on the pullbacks with bigger positions at the places where small STOP LOSS is needed. Don't wait for an ideal prices, because you can miss the TREND.

Trader must analyze every situation from Bullish and Bearish perspective. Every second at the market exist possibilities for Bulls/Bears. The money comes for traders, whose manage their risk properly.
BUY from the top Stop loss must be below previous LOW, BUY at the Double Bottom with small risk and 1:1 reward. At this place it is possible to take bigger position. Triple bottom signal has formed and nice signal bar confirmed possible BUY entry. BUY with 1:1 ratio, because it is position in direction of the main trend. Possibilities are in your favor. Every candle after signal candle, confirm possible BUY opportunities. If you miss signal bar and didn't see it, you can BUY after next candle, don't need to wait for correction or ideal price. If wider stop loss is needed, BUY with smaller position, but bear in mind that minimum risk/reward must be no less than 1:1.

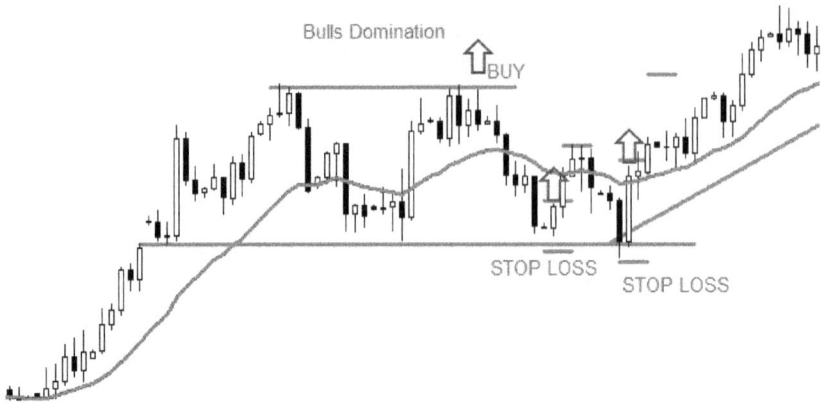

BUY after every Bulls candle. Bulls domination, don't look for trend reversal signal, even Strong Bears signal candle. 70-80 percent of attempts to reverse the trend are false signals. Keep your positions in direction of the trend.

A common mistake with newer traders who attempt multiple timeframe analysis is try to find alignment of trend on all timeframes. They try to identify an uptrend on all three or four timeframes (or a downtrend on all three timeframes) and then trade only in the direction of that trend. This seriously limits opportunity, while still being rather ineffective. We need to see bigger picture, but don't miss opportunities in micro trends also. Trend reversal usually happens near the magnetic zone in bigger time frame. My recommendation is to see higher time frame on H1 or H4 Chart, trading time frame H1 or M15, find entries and exits of orders in

M15 or M5, sometimes in M1 chart. These time frames analysis help us to find low risk entries and follow price action more closely.

At this chart the same situation. There is no difference what chart do you use – Apple, SP500, Dollar index, Oil, EUR/USD, GBPUSD… Bears attempted to reverse the trend and Bulls came back to the market and continue domination. Price Action difference from other systems is universality. No differences that chart analyze – ability to accept right decisions on the right time, read the market tape.

The trading timeframe is the one we trade. Our aim is to trade the swings within this trading timeframe, regardless of whether the market is trending or ranging sideways. To do that for us helps understanding of past price movement, determining the strength or weakness within that price movement and determining the likely path for future price action. The market is fractal structure – the same behavior exists in all time frames – no difference M1, M5, or larger time frame. If I show you the chart and don't reveal that chart it is, you can't say me – is it Apple, Sp500 or EUR/USD chart. The same price behavior or characteristics for all financial instruments, all time frames. We just choose instrument we want to trade, larger picture time frame, trading time frame for entry to the market.

The farther the trend exists, more bears try to reverse the market. A lot of attempts fail. At this chart we can buy even the price is on the highest points, because bulls dominate at the market. After correction – better position, where it is possible to take bigger position. Bears aim to catch up Lower High or Double Top. At this chart we can see big Bears bar near the top – strong signal candle. If choose to trade against the trend at this situation, I need to know that the odds are in not my favor – only 35-40 percent. Also I need to get 2:1 or more. Is it possible at this chart? If you choose to place SELL position, Stop loss must be above the signal candle, profit opportunity only 1:1, because bulls will come back at the bottom with Low risk and greater probabilities.

What's the reason not BUY at this place? Bulls dominate at the market, BUY even the price is so high, don't try to look for SELL signals until Bears don't take over full control from Bulls.

If the market price breaks a trend line or 20EMA, traders usually waiting for:

Sell – Outs or huge Buy backs at the direction of the trend.

New Bottom at the uptrend or new TOP at the downtrend - 70 percent or more is rejected. Sometimes we can see Full Trend Reversal opportunities. Trend reversal minimal requirements at the Uptrend: Lower Low – 1st signal (usually the price come back to the trend. So at this point you must see opportunities to BUY after Signal candle formation with 1:1 ratio). Lower High – 2nd signal (Bears formed Lower High). Lower Low – 3rd signal. Bears took SELL position from Lower high and earned more than 2:1. That's possible signal of Trend Reversal.

Never try to catch up the Trend Reversal earlier than the market dictates you.

At this chart you can see nice bear Trend. The price moves in a channel. Channels rarely look perfect, when drawing just look for best fit. Traders whose like to trade against the trend (they are negative feedback players at the market), Looks for BUY signal from the bottom line. The odds are not in your favor, don't look for a trend reversal signal too early. Signal candle for Bulls looks nice, but context is not supportive. 4 bars in a row formed higher highs, 3 consecutive Bull Bars shows us bullish strength, big bull bodies, it looks good Bulls pressure. Experienced traders understand this price action movement as an opportunity to catch up next selloff near Double TOP. The biggest Bull Bar near the Double Bottom – nice Bulls Trap, it is the candle where crowd comes to the market and believes in trend reversal. Professional Players there see opportunity to SELL with Small risk after signal candle formation and reward 1:1. That's enough, because the trade is higher probability (in direction of the Trend).

Don't Look for BUY signal

After Strong Breakout against the Trend, Bulls are willing to see Higher

LOW or Double Bottom opportunity to BUY, because they believe in a Trend Reversal. Bear in mind, 70-80 percent of attempts to reverse the Trend fail. Bears are waiting for Lower High and at the places where bulls Stop Losses were places, downside movement become more and more active. SELL.

Don't Look for BUY signal

Bears dominate at the market. Only look for sell and don't wait for ideal prices. Consecutive Bear candles in a row, bear candles closes near the lowest point, every Bulls attempt to go to the market, Bears overlap.

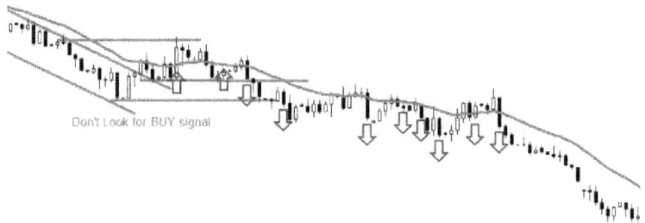

Don't Look for BUY signal

12 Sep 2014 12 Sep 2014 1 Oct 2014 10 Oct 2014 19 Oct 2014 29 Oct 2014 7 Nov 2014 17 Nov 2014 26 Nov 2014 5 Dec 2014 15 Dec 2014 24 Dec 2014 4 Jan 2015 13

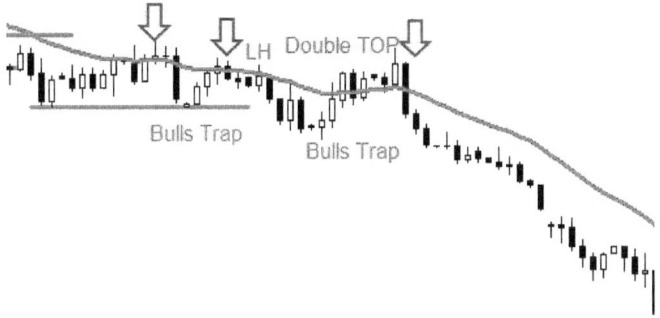

Every time you are looking at the charts, read them from Bullish and Bearish perspective. If you choose to enter to the market against the trend, the odds are not in your favor (35-40 percent probability). If you choose in direction of the Trend – 55-65 percent probability. Calculate possible risk/reward.

At this chart you can determine market phase easily – it is Interval. BUY LOW, SELL HIGH setup. Do this upside movement is similar to Strong Uptrend? It is wave in Interval. First breakout from the LOW to the upside, after some time correction and low inclination angle of upside movement shows us weak Bulls trend. At the middle of the Interval, probabilities are equal for Bulls and Bears (50/50). As far as the price goes closer to the highest point of the Interval, the higher probabilities for Bears. Look for Trend Reversal at the TOP, near magnetic ZONE. At the examples that I showed before, it was Strong Trend market phase, but there is Bull Wave in Interval.

Bulls Interval at the tradable time frame. Look for SELL opportunities at the High of the Channel. Wait for Bulls exhaustion. One of the biggest Bull candles near the TOP (magnetic resistance zone) – potential Bulls Trap. After that Signal candle – Entry with 2:1 and more ratio. Possibilities are in Bears favor.

If we are in Interval Phase, don't believe that the price goes down aggressively without corrections. Channel with low inclination angle or Interval means equal chances both for bulls and bears. Bulls try to from Higher LOW. Bears hold the TOP – Double TOP signal, after some time HL, Triple TOP. Sell High with 2:1 ratio. Bears took control from Bulls when the price broke HL.

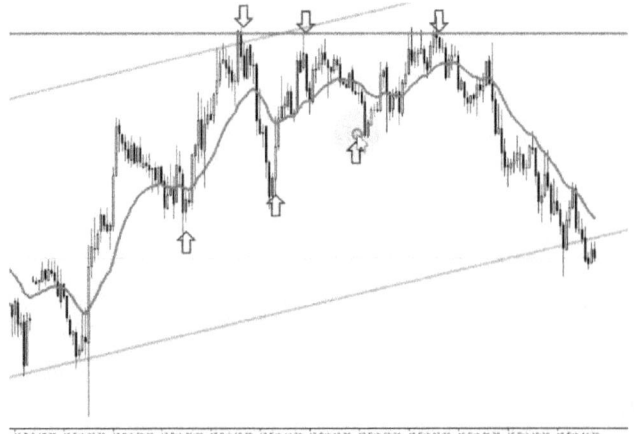

What do you do if the price breaks the micro Bear Channel? Always try to modulate possible price action scenarios. As we see in the higher time frame, this Bear channel is in Interval market cycle, for that reason there is possibility to see breakout of the channel to the upside. Bears waiting for Lower High or Double TOP. SELL High signal will be better and the odds will be in your favor. After the bears take profit with 1:1 ratio, Bulls will try to form Higher LOW or double Bottom. Don't take a temptation to BUY, it is against the direction, the odds are not in your favor. Skip possible BUY opportunities, find Traps for Bulls and SELL at the highs (lower Highs).

At this Chart you can see Strong Bulls domination at the market. After Trend line breakout, few Bear bars and the price stopped, new Low and Bullish consolidation. Bulls are waiting for opportunities to BUY at the Double Bottom signal. BUY LOW with 1:1 ratio. The odds are in your favor. Bears see perspective at the high. It is order against the trend, if on the higher time frame the price is not near the magnetic resistance, don't look for trend reversal. Every Bear bar is overlapped by Bulls, Higher Low has formed and after some time Bulls fully took over control. Only BUY.

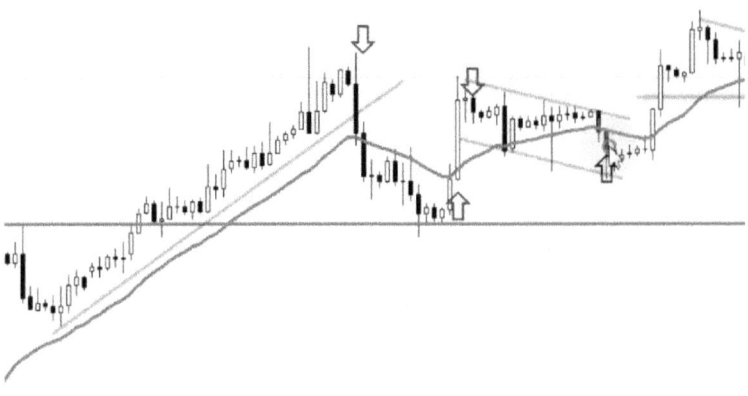

At the bear trend, not importance that financial instrument, every Bulls attempt to take over control was not successful.

The market is a fractal structure – the same behavior exists in all time frames – no difference M1, M5, or larger time frame. If I show you the chart and don't reveal that chart it is, you can't say me – is it Apple, Sp500 or EUR/USD chart. The same price behavior or characteristics for all financial instruments, all time frames. We just choose instrument we want to trade, larger picture time frame, trading time frame for entry to the market.

Higher time frame analysis helps us to determine and identify Strongest

Support and Resistance zones, which act as barriers to trading time frame price moves. Trading time frame (usually I choose M15) is for determining the trend and do assumptions of the future price action movements. Entry to the market and follow price action after order was executed, choose Lower time frame (M5). True mastery is not so much defined by a flawless understanding of price action principles but more by how much a trader is able to do what needs to be done. For the true master will not be affected by whatever happens in a chart. Mentally strong trader will enter his positions unconcerned and exit them without any sense of discomfort. Experienced trader knows that every trade is just one of many. He knows the odds to favor his strategy, but he does not expect to win. His main expectation is to manage the whole process and results will come itself.

8. MENTAL PREPARATION IN TRADING

My personal Price Action system started to give me fruits only after a detailed analysis of emotional intelligence. Mental preparation helped me to survive at the markets firstly, after some time it became natural to make money at the markets. Trading is as a business, you need to be prepared and have knowledge base of market character and crowd psychology.
You are Trading well when you are following your Trading Plan. Trader who does not trade well is making lots of mistakes, usually psychological. If he does not take corrective action according to his Trading Plan, he will never leave the game with profit on a consistent basis. You can always change your Trading Plan if you don't realize acceptable profit, but if you don't Trade Well, you are lost! Don't trade since you are not prepared mentally. My advice from personal way to success – every setup in trading look from Price Action, Money Management and Psychological perspective.

When emotional intelligence first appeared to the masses, it served as the missing link in a peculiar finding: people with average IQs outperform those with the highest IQs 70% of the time. This anomaly threw a massive wrench into what many people had always assumed was the sole source of success—IQ. Decades of research now point to emotional intelligence as the critical factor that sets star performers apart from the rest of the pack. Emotional intelligence is the "something" in each of us that is a bit intangible. It affects how we manage behavior, navigate social complexities, and make personal decisions that achieve positive results. Emotional intelligence is made up of four core skills that pair up under two primary competencies: personal competence and social competence. For traders the most important is Personal Competence. **Personal competence** comprises your self-awareness and self-management skills, which focus more on you individually than on your interactions with other people. Personal competence is your ability to stay aware of your emotions and manage your behavior and tendencies. Self-Awareness is your ability to accurately perceive your emotions and stay aware of them as they happen.

Self-Management is your ability to use awareness of your emotions to stay flexible and positively direct your behavior.

Intelligence is your ability to learn, but emotional intelligence, on the other hand, is a flexible set of skills that can be acquired and improved with practice. You can develop high emotional intelligence even if you aren't born with it. Students, whose become good traders and professional traders I personally know, all of them are not genius or with high IQ. Emotional intelligence research companies have done a lot of analysis and they found that 90 percent of top performers are also high in emotional intelligence. Some of them have it naturally, some of them acquire. Just 20 percent of bottom performers have high emotional intelligence. You can be top performer without high Emotional intelligence, but chances are slim. The same chances as believe in profits in trading against the trend. It doesn't matter how we name that – emotional intelligence or mental preparation, it is very important part of traders life.

I personally during all my trading day, ask myself a lot of questions before decision, it helps me to keep my trading plan and listen to the market. Emotions become more rational in our trading if we have Trading Plan. My Trading Plan is based on Assumptions. Every time when you trade, make assumptions, try to imagine probability, decide position size and define the market phase.

Every second the market offers opportunities for Bulls and Bears, but money makes only trader who better understand the market and entry the market at the better places, logical position sizes and stop loss sizes. Traders, whose control the price action methodology, don't wait for an ideal place at the market, don't believe in fast profits, and don't feel fear of loss. They are emotionally stronger, that I mean mental prepared. My trading plan incorporates the knowledge and implementation of money and self-management, market phase analysis (context), Assumptions, Dominant Force (Bulls/Bears), Market Entry and exit time frame selection. Usually, I select to entry the market at the smaller time frame, but exit at the larger time frame. This is for a better money management.

Markets are largely subjected to the human factor. Technical intelligence is not enough in efficient trading. Control your emotions and understand how other people emotions affect their trading decisions. If you have an experience at the markets, I suppose you understand the importance of Emotional intelligence and self-management. Every day as a trader you must start from zero. The market doesn't remember that happened yesterday, every day is unique. It is not important how much profit/loss yesterday you made. Forget that and look at the charts with clear mind. One of the most important error trader makes is that they are looking for ultra-high probability strategies. If a trader has 90 percentage hit, don't look at his trading as an example. Holy Grail doesn't exist, because if it would be real methodology, everyone use it and after some time it will fail. Imagine – everyone starts to BUY, whose take SELL orders? Every system or methodology every time must be improving, updating.

Successful traders always try to do assumptions and ask question: ,,What probability of success in that trade is?''

One of the main things that affect our emotionally not stable stance during the trading, is that the odds are unknown. I personally do assumptions and that helps me to do better, rational decisions, be mentally prepared in every trade. Must people hate uncertain future. They feel lost in the fog. This feeling spoils their life, we live in a world that brings uncertainty and realities are far from being totally known. People tend to be afraid of what they don't know to be afraid of. Trader expectations must be realistic and as much as more realistic they are, more confidence comes to trading. Better to choose the orders that are with higher probabilities than low probabilities. High probability entries mean trading in direction of the Trend. The odds are 55-60 percent. If you are trading against the trend, the odds are 35-40 percent. So it is not in your favor. If you choose to trade low probability Entries, money management must compensate low probability. Minimal profit/loss ratio must be no less than 2:1 or more. Why do you need to risk your money if the odds are not in your favor? Only one reason – if it is great profit opportunity (2:1 or more). If you trade in direction of the Trend, the odds are in your favor. So reward/risk 1:1 is enough. My advice is not to trade less than 1:1 ratio. If you trade less than 1:1 ratio, your probabilities must be near 70 percent of time. Not lot professionals have consistent probability of 70 percent for a long time. Choose the trades that have better probability. Don't be afraid of the 35-40 percent probability of failure. If you want to become successful trader, you must be reconciled with unknown environment.

One more reason of feelings is the embarrassing past or present. People tend to prefer pleasurable impressions to painful ones. Forget past failures or existing risk at the market. The market hasn't memory. Every single day starts from zero. There are 3 the most important things in trading: 1.

Probability, 2. Reward, 3. Risk.

We can't control the probabilities, but we can manage the risk and reward. That's our strength. What is risk? Risk is the length of pips till the STOP LOSS. Reward is quantity of the pips till your take profit. What is the most important? From the first look, the most important is Probability. That's the reason why make money at the markets is not easy. But it is not the most important thing from professional look. Probabilities for new traders interfere to take the best potential orders at the market. Also they tend to leave the market too early, fix small profits instead of maximize. The odds and uncertain environment causes the emotions at the market. And that's the reason also why to trade the market for me is one of the most interesting occupations in life. Always try to find an apparently rational / logical explanation for a behavior which is just instinctive or emotional. Don't allow emotions to take over control of your brains. Your goal is to trade rational. Imagine extreme sports – do you think the people whose are doing that don't feel fear? They feel, but they manage their emotions. The markets are environment where you can improve your emotional intelligence skills and that helps you in all life. Not only brings profits in your trading, but also do your life more better. At the markets there are a lot of High frequency trading, computers don't have emotions. You can earn the money only if follow them. You can't earn the money if you are not free from your emotions. Probabilities are always unknown, but that's the reason why for us the most important thing is money management. Uncertainty is everywhere in human life as well as in the Universe. Risk tries to tame uncertainty by adding arithmetic (probabilities). People are rather risk averse. They accept risk normally only if it brings above normal benefit prospect. The same is in trading. I like one phrase that I heard from one trader: financial markets and financial institutions are dedicated "shops" where you can buy and sell risks and return prospects.

Probabilities can't be known, for that reason we are doing assumptions. For decision making, to be conscious of risks and uncertainties, and to see how they are balanced by prospective rewards are crucial. Our probabilities are subjective - we just create possible scenarios and hypothesis. For me it is always reliable approach is to do assumptions from personal experience in trading Price Action. The probabilities depend on market phase or context. If we are in trending environment – 55-60 percent of success, if against the trend – 35-40 percent if Interval market phase 50/50 – equal bulls and bears. That view helps to do better money management decisions. If we see good entry signal and it fits our trading plan, the highest probability is near 60 percent. No more, don't believe that probability is higher than 60 percent. It is for psychological status. It helps not to be overconfident in trading. If you can't determine market phase, the greatest probability that you can expect is 50 percent. In that situation profit must be 2 times higher than loss. Comparing risk (uncertainty) to potential rewards is one of the bases of decision making. Remember, that the higher the risk taken, the higher the benefits should be. This rule valid in trading against the trend the most.

There exists one mental status that means false certainties. False certainties in matters which are uncertain are beliefs and illusions. They might be based either on a lack of knowledge or attention. Your mental strength improves when master price action, market behavior and psychology. There are no guarantees in trading. It is business of probabilities. Try to develop your trading decisions every trading day. Every time you entry the market, make sure that profit/loss ratio is no less than 1:1.

Financial markets and financial institutions are shops where risks as well as return prospects can be bought or sold. They tend to ask an additional return for risky investment compared to those that are considered riskless. If the risk is greater than possible return, you should be more than

70 percent of times right if you want to be with zero in long term. An ideal entries don't exist. It is impossible to be right for Bulls and Bears at the same time, they can't win both at the same time.

I think that I demonstrate you that emotional intelligence is crucial in trading decisions. Every trading day analyze not only markets, but also yourself, manage not only orders, but also mental strength or psychology. Train yourself in live market situation, not only from the past. Try to improve your decisions making habits every day.

A basic Emotional Intelligence skill for traders also involves using the appropriate emotions to aid in decision making. When trader studying the markets after the close, he uses low energy emotion. And that helps to concentrate maximum attention to the charts. When trader sees live charts in front of his and does decision in real market environment, he uses high resources of emotions. Emotional intelligent trader will acknowledge feelings that a trade isn't a great prospect even setup may meet price action criteria, rules. As the emotion surges, we are likely to act rashly, only to regret it later, or feel ashamed or embarrassed when the things calm down. Always try to do assumptions in trading determine market phase, know your potential on that situation, determine risks, reward. Remember, uncertain environment is normal in all our lives. Trading environment can't provide you guarantees or Holy Grail. That perception will help you to be more emotionally stable Keep attention and focus at the market price is good drug for your emotional intelligence. Don't fear to be wrong. During the trading decision-making time, you can afford no interruptions. If your office is in your home and you trade intraday, get a lock to separate yourself from anyone sharing the premises and use it. If this presents a problem with your wife or family, don't trade. Maximal concentration and focus to the charts every trading day.

9. PREQUSITIES, TRADING PLAN

You should understand that this is not a book on basic technical analysis. It is a book about a modular and comprehensive trading approach that I have found to be both prudent and highly effective. For that reason my book mission is to teach you high performance price action trading strategies. I love that I do every trading day, also my mission is to share my knowledge with you. I suppose you will find and apply information in your trading day.

At this section I will try to explain you perquisites and create trading plan. Why do you need to have trading plan? Because emotions are important part in our decisions making process. There is no room for jealously, envy, emotional insecurity. If you suffer significantly from any of the personality flaws mentioned above, you are not stable emotionally, first iron out those flaws, then learn about trading specifics. Trading plan and good understanding of rules helps you to trade more disciplined.

How much currency pairs or financial instruments do you need to monitor?

For me, it is better to trade not only one financial instrument. Sometimes in one instrument you just see that context is not supportive for entering the market. But there is good potential in other financial instrument. My recommendation for you : choose chart for trading at the existing day where you can determine the context the best and see the best reward/risk opportunities. Remind my phrase that I mentioned in the past sections: ,, Financial markets are shops where risks as well as return prospects can be bought or sold. "

Always try to ask yourself this question:

Does existing price movement the Trend? If yes, only look for BUY/SELL opportunities in that direction. You can courage to say that market phase TREND. Proper money management should be 1:1, never trade with less reward/risk ratio.

More complicated market phase is if your answer to this question would be: no, it is only up/down wave in Interval. You are in Interval market phase. You trading plan: BUY LOWS, SELL highs. The odds are equal for both sides. Find the highest magnet ant the lowest magnet. Also draw middle zone. Probabilities are equal in middle zone, the greater chances are near the top/bottom. Mark possible projections. If the market breaks the middle zone of existing chart, it becomes the lowest/highest magnet for new Interval in higher time frame.

The market always is moving in Interval. For me the best to choose H4 chart for determining market phase, H1 chart for determining possible entry points, determine probabilities and M15/M5 chart for entries. For example, if I determine that existing price action in H4 chart is Up/Down wave in Interval, H1 chart helps me to see the Interval Closer. Also I see how much existing wave is far from middle zone, determine the odds for BUY LOW SELL high trading plan. After that I open M15 or M5 chart for enter to the market. If I see micro trend in Interval and there is a lot of space till the lowest/highest point of magnet, I can capitalize opportunities of micro trend. As much closer the price comes to Magnet, the greater the chances to see Trend Reversal. In that situation M15 chart or M5 chart I use for enter the market with Trend Reversal signal. Determine the odds and based on that reward/risk profile. If you entered a trade on the basis of some criteria and that criteria is negated, you don't look around for other criteria to justify your position. If you do, you have made a serious Mistake. Close the trade, and if you have other criteria to be in the trade, re-open it, on that basis. Bear in mind also lesson about the signal bar detection. Entry the market only after signal bar formation and then the price breaks the extreme of signal bar.

My idea how to create your individual Trading Plan in your brains or excel:

Market Phase time Frame: Daily or H4
Determine possible entry point: H1 chart
Entry signal Chart: M15 chart
Highest Magnet price:
Lowest Magnet price:
Middle zone:
Possibilities:
Reward/Risk ratio:
Psychological condition: Uncertainty/ Clarity

Let's look at this Daily GOLD chart:

Market Phase: Interval. The price near the middle zone. Probability equal for both bulls and bears for longer term trade. If you enter BUY position at this point, your stop loss must be below lowest magnet and take profit near the highest. So 1:1 ratio, probability 50/50. Is it good entry for longer term trade? No.

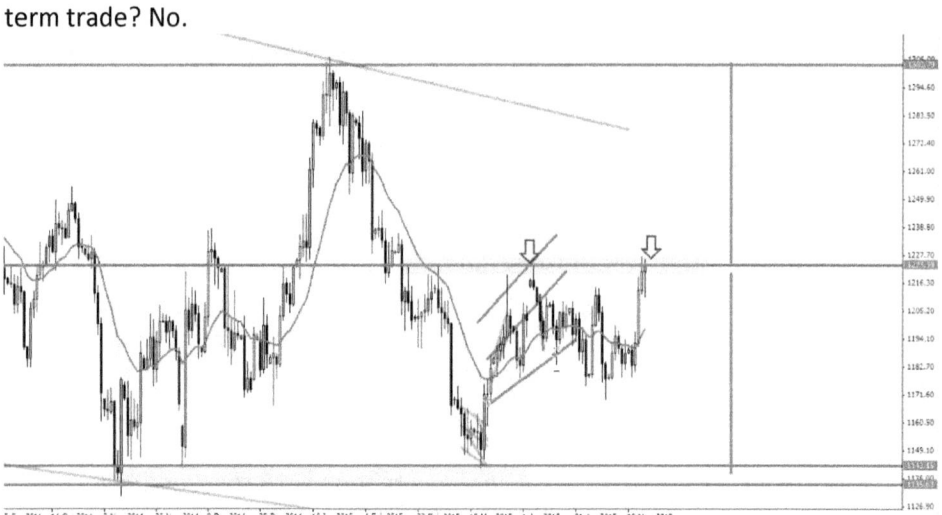

H4 chart:
Market Phase: Interval. The price is near the TOP – highest Magnet. Probabilities for short term trade is near 55 percent for bears. How we know probability? It is only assumption that we are doing based on experience. What Reward/Risk can offer the trade for me at this price? 2:1 or more

H1 Chart:

Market Phase: We see only one trend in the screen. It is micro Trend. What we need to do at this chart? Waiting for confirmation of that Short term Micro trend reversal:

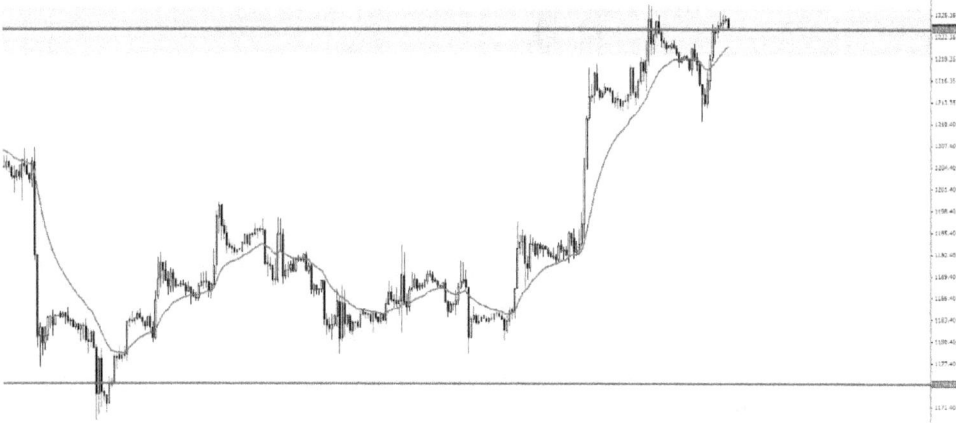

M15 Chart: Looking for the best Entry point with 2:1 and more: Interval Price action. The price is near the highest point of Interval. Possibilities in your favor – 2:1 reward/risk ratio.

The same Chart. Entry signal. Psychological status: clarity. Clear reward/Risk ratio, probabilities in your favor:

Alternative Scenario: If the price breaks the middle zone, it will be signal that it will be able to wait for up movement to 1300 – the highest Magnet. As closer the price goes to the TOP magnet, the faster price moves to that level. So we will have micro Uptrend. And at the H4, H1 chart it will be UPTREND market Phase. Probabilities will be 55-60 percent for bulls. The closer the price will be near the TOP, the greater chances to see bigger correction at H1 or M15 uptrend chart. Look for Trend Reversal only near the highest magnet. If the price penetrates the highest Magnet, it becomes the middle zone of the bigger Interval. Remember – the price always moves in Interval.

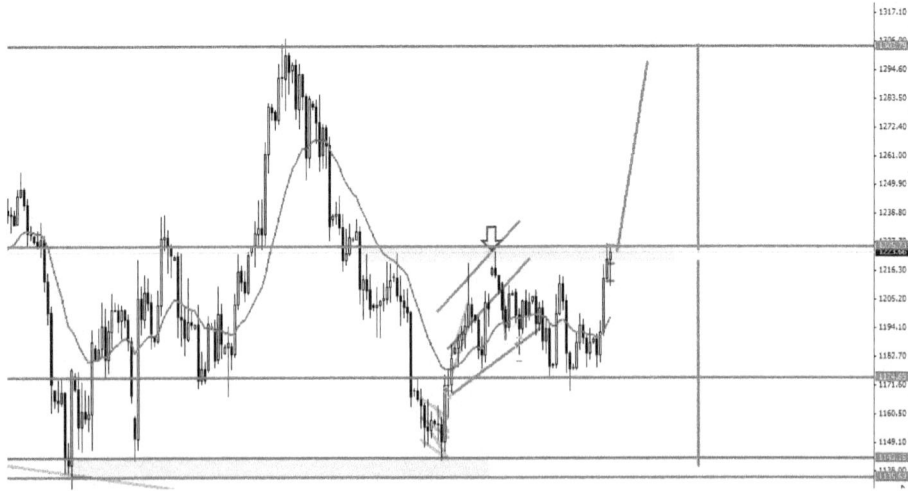

Psychological preparation importance:

I mentioned a lot in all book sections about risk management importance, but true key is your individual psychology. What's the main components that prevent traders from becoming consistently successful? That's lack of methodology, discipline, unrealistic expectations and lack of patience. Before starting your trading career it is critical to understand your personal psychology – how it can affect your trading?

Trading Methodology: your simple, clear, rules and probabilities, capital management based way of looking at the markets. Lack of trading methodology means that you don't have a way to know what constitutes BUY or SELL signal.

Try to write down methodology: as my recommendation was to do your own trading journal in your brains or written. If you can't fit on few sentences, it is too complicated. Remember magical question: What I see on the chart? Is this Upside/Downside movement a TREND or just wave in Interval?

Lack of Discipline: if your view at a price chart or evaluate a potential trade setup today is different from how you did it month ago, then you either have not identified your methodology or just lack of discipline to follow the methodology you have identified. If you want to get results from the trading, you must consistently apply a proven methodology.

Lack of patience: Remember – markets trend only about 30 percent of time, other 70 percent of the time the markets are in non-trending environment. For that reason the tops and bottoms are definitely where the risk is smallest and the profit potential is greatest. Someone is trading in those areas, selling at the tops and buying at the bottoms. For the reason, that there are long periods of non-trending market environment, if you are long tern trader, only two or three compelling tradable moves present themselves during the year. If you are short term trader, there are setups for trading every day, every week, you just need to find the best entries.

Trading is really exciting , because involves money. For that reason lot of traders feel that missing something if they are not in in a trade. For that reason setups of trading becomes lesser and lesser quality and means overtrading. Don't worry about missing of opportunity today, because there are opportunities and will be later.

How to overcome the tendency to be impatient? You must understand the two triggers that cause: fear and boredom. How to overcome impatience? My advice would be: determine minimum requirements of an acceptable trade setup. If your goal is to be consistently successful trader, the most important thing is setup quality, not quantity. Consistently successful trading is not easy. As a trader, you must have realistic expectations. First year should be to avoid of losing money. After some time you will generate returns and become successful trader. I suppose my book will help you to reach your goals and become better trader.

For more information visit my personal website. Subscribe my newsletter with insights about price action:

www.highperformancepriceaction.com

ABOUT THE AUTHOR

Dainius Šilkaitis is experienced (10 years), independent full-time trader, who is well-versed in Price Action analysis, founded unique high performance price action trading methodology. Dainius in his trading combines sentiment, fundamental analysis and trading setups based on price action. He occasionally writes for trading and investment publications in most well-known Lithuanian websites. In this book Dainius reveals personal breakthroughs in trading Price Action and that is different look at the market. Price Action following system help for traders understand price behaviour and to see what professional traders we seeing at the market that novice or beginner couldn't see.

Dainius is the creator of the Advanced Price Action FX course, Fundamental/Sentiment trading course which is designed for both new and intermediate traders to jump-start their trading performance. Dainius has mentored hundreds of independent traders.

Get more information, trading ideas from Dainius Šilkaitis:

www.highperformancepriceaction.com

www.ingramcontent.com/pod-product-compliance
Lightning Source LLC
Chambersburg PA
CBHW051918170526
45168CB00001B/447